Amazing Horse
Facts and Trivia

Amazing
Horse
Facts and Trivia

An illustrated guide to the equine world

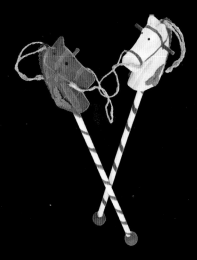

Gary Mullen

CHARTWELL
BOOKS, INC.

A QUARTO BOOK

Published in 2008 by
CHARTWELL BOOKS, INC.
A division of BOOK SALES, INC.
276 Fifth Avenue Suite 206
New York, New York 10001
USA

Copyright © 2008 Quarto Inc.
Reprinted in 2010 (twice), 2011 (twice),
2012, 2013

ISBN-13: 978-0-7858-2456-5
ISBN-10: 0-7858-2456-1

Conceived, designed,
and produced by
Quarto Publishing plc
The Old Brewery
6 Blundell Street
London N7 9BH

QUA: HFLT

Editor & designer:
Michelle Pickering
Proofreader: Julia Halford
Indexer: Dorothy Frame
Art director: Caroline Guest
Illustrator: Kang Kuo Chen

Creative director: Moira Clinch
Publisher: Paul Carslake

Color separation by Modern Age
Repro House Ltd., Hong Kong
Printed by Midas Printing
International Ltd., China

Contents

**The contents of this book are completely random, so that
each time you open it, you will be surprised by a wonderful
variety of amazing facts and trivia about the equine world.
If you wish to locate a particular category of information,
however, this contents listing is organized into helpful
topics. You will also find a detailed index on pages 186–191.**

Introduction 6

PHYSICAL CHARACTERISTICS

CARE, OWNERSHIP & USES

CASUAL SHOES FOR MINIATURES

Miniature Horses are finding their niche as seeing-eye service animals. Wearing tennis shoes helps to prevent their feet from getting chipped and worn on hard surfaces.

A Miniature Horse from the Guide Horse Foundation in North Carolina.

The average horse stands at about 15–15½ hands high—60–62 inches (152–157 cm).

THE WORLD'S SMALLEST HORSE
Thumbelina is the smallest horse on record, measuring a mere 17 inches (43 cm) at five years of age. That is only a little over 4.1 hands tall. She is a dwarf Miniature Horse. Most adult Miniature Horses are 28–34 inches (71–86 cm) tall. Only 10 pounds (4.5 kg) at birth, Thumbelina now weighs 60 pounds (27 kg).

THE WORLD'S TALLEST HORSE

The documented record holder for height is a Belgian Draft gelding called Radar from Mt. Pleasant, Texas, at 19.3 hands ½ inch tall—6 feet 7½ inches (2.02 m). There are unofficial records, dating from 1904, of a horse measuring over 21 hands—84 inches (2.13 m).

Can Horses Vomit?
No, because a muscular valve that leads to the stomach prevents food from going back into the esophagus, making it almost impossible to vomit.

MISCELLANEOUS FACTS

INTRODUCTION

At the age of ten, I was given my first equine ... a fat, obnoxious pony named Sherry that my father acquired in trade for a table saw. She would throw me to the ground on a regular basis, and was the start of my equine education via the school of hard knocks. Forty years later, I can appreciate Sherry and other amazing equines—the ones that brought me awards as a child; the ones that garnered me national championships as an adult; the ones I trained in order to pay my way through three universities and provide for a family of eight. Through the years, horses have served me, encouraged me (better than any therapist could), and strengthened me, promoting self-discipline, industry, patience, and responsibility. Yes, horses are truly amazing; hopefully, that is what this book will clearly reveal to you.

This book should serve as a valuable resource for those who are new to the world of horses, as well as professional horsemen who want an educational tool for their clients and perhaps themselves. Every interesting question I have asked over the years has been answered in this book—I wish I had this information forty years ago! Besides a plethora of amazing horse facts, feats, and trivia, you will get an overview of the horse industry, including information about equine terms, breeds, history, competitions, safety, buying, riding, health care, and management.

The lighthearted, eclectic design of the book is for your reading enjoyment. Refer to the listing of topics in the contents at the front of the book, or the index at the back of the book, when a particular question arises and you want to locate the answer. I always seem to forget horse vital signs, and various horse facts, figures, and terms. This book should serve as an excellent reference source for forgetful people like me.

Enjoy the book as much as I already have from "living it" and putting it into written form. May you, through reading this book, realize that a fat, obnoxious pony is actually a beautiful and amazing creation.

A horse's lips are designed for grasping.

Count the Cost

Buying a horse, or getting one for free, is the easy part. Ownership involves regular expenditures on board (room and feed), training, lessons, horse shoeing (every 6–8 weeks), vet care, tack, and supplies, as well as countless hours of responsibility. A wise saying is, "It's not the cost of the horse that is the concern. It's the upkeep."

Stiff Upper Lip
Equines have a sensitive, prehensile upper lip. Prehensile means it is adapted for feeling, grasping, and seizing objects, such as grass.

Hobby Horse

The hobby horse, or stick horse, is a horse head on a broomstick, popular in the 18th and 19th centuries as a toy. The expression "to ride one's hobby horse" means to follow a favorite pastime—hence now known as a hobby.

Hobby is an old word for a type of strong, active horse.

DO GLUE FACTORIES EXIST?

Even though many glues are now synthetic, livestock and horse parts that contain collagen (for example, tendons, ligaments, hooves, and cartilage) are still used to make some glue products. Hoof glue is primarily used for woodworking.

REALLY WILD

The last remaining true wild horse is Przewalski's Horse (also known as the Asiatic Wild Horse, Mongolian Wild Horse, or Takhi). Scientists disagree on its species classification. These wild horses have 66 chromosomes, whereas domestic horses have 64. The wild horse can breed with the domestic horse, producing fertile offspring with 65 chromosomes. When Przewalski's Horse neared extinction in the early 1900s, the Zoological Society of London worked with Mongolian scientists to preserve them in zoos, building the population to a point where over 250 are again living in the wild in Mongolia. A recent census reports approximately 1,500 in existence.

The Centaur is a symbol of the astrological sign Sagittarius.

AN ODD CROSSBREED

The Centaur was a mythological creature that was half-man on top, with the body of a horse. Centaurs had a reputation for being savage. Their meals were said to be double-portioned—one meal for the human part, and one meal for the horse part.

A Przewalski's Horse grazing.

Equestrian
The term equestrian refers to someone who rides horses.

Le Carrousel

* The earliest known carousel is depicted in a Byzantine bas-relief from around A.D. 500, showing riders suspended in baskets from a central pole.

* European Crusaders used the word carousel— from the Italian *garosello* and Spanish *carosella* (little war)—to describe a combat training exercise performed by Turkish and Arabian horsemen in the 1100s.

* The Crusaders took the idea of the carousel back home, where it was used for secret training within the castle walls of the ruling lords and kings.

* Eventually, carousels for entertainment appeared. La Place du Carrousel in Paris was so-named because of the pageants and games that took place there, with knights competing in a variety of contests.

* Although horses are the usual mounts nowadays, others include deer, dogs, cats, pigs, and rabbits.

Antique carousel horse

WORLD'S MOST EXPENSIVE HORSE?

In 2006, a 2-year-old Thoroughbred race colt was purchased at auction for $16 million (£8 million) by a London-based horse breeding and training operation. In order to recover the purchase price, the colt will need to supplement his racing income with breeding fees that could be close to $50,000 (£25,000) per breeding.

One-sided Horses

Some of the world's most ornate and expensive carousel horses have much less detail on the side that is less visible.

Mmmm! Tasty!

Eating Dirt and Wood

✦ Horses occasionally eat dirt or wood.

✦ Possible causes include boredom; the need for more fiber (hay); self-medication (taking in soil microbes that help absorb toxins and viruses); or self-supplementation of missing nutrients (e.g. salt, minerals).

✦ Foals might nibble on manure as they learn what is appropriate to eat.

SAND EATERS

Many horses ingest sand while grazing, increasing the risk of colic (stomach ache). Psyllium is a fiber product that, when fed to the horse, is believed to absorb sand and help it pass through the intestines.

Double trouble—eating sand and wood.

DAPPLES = GOOD HEALTH?

Dapples (dark-colored circle outlines) on a gray horse are considered attractive, especially in the competition arena. Dapples are just a beautiful color pattern on some gray horses, some Buckskins, and some other colors. Occasionally, dark-colored horses have textured dapples that are similar to texture differences on a fabric. What causes these faint circles on a horse's coat? Many believe them to be a sign of a healthy horse, but that is a controversial theory. Some believe them to be genetic and not related to good health at all.

VERBAL CUES

• Horses can be encouraged to move or stop by the use of verbal cues, such as "walk," "trot," "canter," or "whoa," or clicking and clucking sounds.

• Harsh sounds are intimidating, and soft tones can be relaxing.

• If you want to appear knowledgeable, do not say "giddy up" when asking a horse to move forward. This term is seldom used by serious horsemen. A "cluck, cluck" will suffice.

Happy birthday to you!

Happy birthday to you!

ONE BIG PARTY

• All Thoroughbreds registered by the Jockey Club celebrate their birthdays on January 1st in the northern hemisphere, and August 1st in the southern hemisphere.

• This birth date keeps horses in age brackets for racing purposes.

• Breeders attempt to have foals born close to the beginning of the year, so that they are as large and strong as their racing peers.

Diving Horses

✦ The famous Atlantic City Steel Pier diving horses were trained to dive from a height of 60 feet (18 m) into a pool that was only 10 feet (3 m) deep. They dove four times a day for seven days a week during the regular show schedule. Reportedly, when the act closed, the last two diving horses were sold to a slaughterhouse, but were saved by a rescue group.

✦ Horse diving became a popular attraction at other amusement parks in the early part of the 20th century, including New York City's Hippodrome and White City Amusement Park, Massachusetts. Horse diving still takes place today at Lake George, New York.

✦ In 1991, Disney made the movie *Wild Hearts Can't Be Broken* about a teenager in the Depression who rode diving horses. Based on a true story, the girl was blinded during a horse-diving accident, but still continued to horse dive.

Horsepower

☆ A UNIT OF HORSEPOWER EQUALS THE POWER NEEDED TO LIFT 165 POUNDS (75 KG) TO A HEIGHT OF 27 INCHES (68.5 CM) IN ONE SECOND.

☆ THE AVERAGE HORSE IS ACTUALLY CAPABLE OF PRODUCING 10–13 UNITS OF HORSEPOWER.

In Colorado on July 4th, 1905, Eunice Winkless dove on horseback into a pool of water from a high tower to win a $100 (£50) challenge.

Some breeders would like to clone their best horses.

Cloning

* In 2003, Italian scientists cloned a horse.

* In 2005, a champion endurance gelding (castrated male) was cloned in the hope that the cloned horse would father future champions.

* The cost to clone a horse is around $150, 000 (£75,000).

* Some breeders are hopeful of duplicating winning racehorses and performance horses.

HOOF OR FOOT?

Either term is acceptable. A famous saying, "No foot, no horse," warns that poorly cared for feet may make a horse lame and worthless, just like a car with a flat tire.

A horse's teeth grow about 1/8 inch (3 mm) a year.

Those Pearly Whites

+ Most female horses have 36 teeth; most males have 40–42 teeth.

+ All horses have 12 incisors (front teeth) that are good for cutting grass, and 24 molars (cheek or jaw teeth) that are good for chewing grass.

+ Some males have canine (fighting) teeth between the molars and incisors.

+ Some males and females have little, sharp wolf teeth in front of their molars. Wolf teeth may need to be removed so that a bit can fit in the horse's mouth painlessly.

+ Horses naturally have a toothless area (bar) between the incisors and molars, at just the right location and size to wear a bit.

+ There are professional vets or horse dentists that float (file) sharp teeth as needed.

+ Foals are usually born toothless, with incisors appearing in approximately 8–10 days.

The direction of horse races varies in different countries.

GOING AROUND IN CIRCLES

Racehorses run counterclockwise in the United States, whereas in Europe they usually run clockwise. Rumor has it that a Kentucky track builder—a staunch supporter of the Revolution—introduced this concept to the U.S. in the late 1700s as a gesture to be different from the British.

EQUINE COLLEGES

* In many countries there are colleges and universities that offer degrees (Associate, Bachelor, Master, and Doctorate) related to different forms of equine studies.

* Students are often able to take their own horses to college with them.

* Intercollegiate riding competitions are becoming as popular as other college team sports.

HORSES IN "THE LORD OF THE RINGS"

HORSE	RIDER(S)
Arod	Legolas and Gimli
Asfaloth	Glorfindel
Bill the Pony	Hobbits of the Fellowship
Bumpkin	Merry Brandybuck
Fatty Lumpkin	Tom Bombadil
Felaróf	Eorl
Firefoot	Eomer
Hasufel	Aragorn (his borrowed horse)
Roheryn	Aragorn (his own horse)
Shadowfax	Gandalf
Sharp-ears	Merry Brandybuck
Snowmane	King Théoden
Strider	Frodo Baggins
Stybba	Merry Brandybuck
Swish-tail	Merry Brandybuck
White-socks	Merry Brandybuck
Windfola	Eowyn
Wise-nose	Merry Brandybuck

Body Language

In the wild, horses use body language to communicate with the rest of the herd. A horse confronted by something frightening or potentially dangerous will analyze the threat and respond according to the perceived seriousness of the danger.

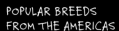

An alert Saddlebred displays the early stages of the startle response.

❶ Startle response: The horse raises its head to look and listen intently. It pricks up its ears and points them forward, flares its nostrils to take in potentially informative smells, and opens its eyes wide to see as much as possible. If it perceives a threat, it may back off in a nervous way and start pawing the ground while still trying to figure out what is going on. It may also snort, raise its tail, and prance about, then either wheel around on its hindlegs and gallop away or stand and face the threat.

THE SADDLEBRED

The Saddlebred is one of the most glamorous horses in the world. Although fiery, spirited, and proud, it is also gentle, with one of the kindest temperaments of any horse. The breed is noted for its intelligence and alertness, as well as its high, exaggerated action.

A Saddlebred snacks on a snowman's nose.

POPULAR BREEDS FROM THE AMERICAS
- Appaloosa
- Assateague and Chincoteague Ponies
- Azteca
- Criollo
- Falabella
- Galiceno
- Gypsy Vanner
- Kiger Mustang
- Mangalarga
- Miniature Horse
- Missouri Fox Trotter
- Morgan
- National Show Horse
- Paint Horse
- Paso Fino
- Peruvian Paso
- Pony of the Americas
- Quarter Horse
- Rocky Mountain Pony
- Saddlebred
- Standardbred
- Tennessee Walking Horse

An angry white horse flattens its ears and advances with its head lowered.

❷ Display of aggression:
If the threat is another horse, it may display aggression. This involves thrusting its head forward, with ears back, nostrils wrinkled up and back, and perhaps baring its teeth. If the threat remains, the horse may move forward, with its head low and neck stretched out, ready to lunge at the threat if necessary.

❸ Attack: If the horse intruder does not withdraw, a fight may ensue. The horses will bite at each other anywhere within reach. Males, in particular, often rear up with flailing forelegs, trying to come down onto the back of their opponent and get them down onto the ground where they can be trampled and kicked. Some horses, particularly mares, may also back into each other, kicking out with their hind feet.

A horse rears up into an aggressive fighting stance.

A mare cleans her newborn foal as it stands for the first time.

Foaling

+ Humans give birth, dogs whelp, cattle calve, sheep lamb, and horses foal.

+ Foaling usually takes around 30 minutes, typically in the night hours or early morning.

LOVER OF HORSES

The Greek name Phillipa (female version of Philip) means lover of horses.

A love of horses has inspired many works of art.

What Makes for a Smooth Ride?

When a horse paces (ambles), it is performing a lateral two-beat gait (pairs of legs on the same side form one beat) rather than a diagonal two-beat gait, as in the trot (diagonal pairs of legs form one beat). The side-to-side motion enables the horse's back to remain very flat and level, thereby creating less bounce and a smoother ride.

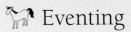 Eventing

★ Three-day eventing, an Olympic event, involves horses and riders competing on three different days in dressage, cross-country jumping, and show jumping.

★ Solid fences (non-forgiving) are used on the cross-country courses, consisting of logs, ditches, water, drops, and so on, all jumped at a fast gallop. Show jumps consist of elements that can be knocked down, thereby earning penalty points (faults).

★ To win the Rolex Grand Slam of Eventing, a rider must win three major competitions in succession: the Rolex Kentucky Three-day Event in the U.S. and the Badminton Horse Trials and Burghley Horse Trials in England. The prize is $250,000 (£125,000) and a gold Rolex watch.

HUNTER VS. JUMPER

Both terms describe jumping horses. In the show arena, jumpers are shown over high and wide jumps, and the winner is the one who has the least amount of faults (knockdown of jumps, and time penalties). Jumpers are not judged on their form, obedience, or rhythm. All they need to do is cleanly get over the fences. Hunters, on the other hand, jump smaller fences, and they are judged on form, obedience, relaxation, and rhythm.

Taking a cross-country jump at the Badminton Horse Trials.

Homework for Horse Buyers

Before you go to check out a horse for purchase, be proactive. Window shopping (impulsive, emotional buying) can be dangerous, so ask these enlightening questions of the seller, over the phone.

1 Has the horse ever colicked or foundered?
2 Has it ever been lame?
3 Has it ever had surgery of any kind?
4 Does it crib?
5 Has it ever been sick?
6 Does it need special shoeing?
7 Has anyone ever been thrown from the horse?
8 Has it ever bucked or reared?
9 If it sits for a couple of days, how does the horse behave?
10 What kinds of things make it spook?
11 Describe what it does when it spooks.
12 Describe the look and feel of its walk, trot, and canter.
13 How does the horse behave on trail rides? How many times has it gone on the trails?
14 How is it when you arrive at a strange place or horse show? Does it need to be lunged to relax?
15 How is it when another horse passes it from behind?
16 Does it ever get tense in a show, or unfamiliar place?
17 How much training does the horse really have? How many times has it been ridden per week, per month?
18 Has it had any time off over the years? How long, and why?

Buying a horse is a huge commitment, so ask lots of questions to help you make the right decision.

19 What is the history of this horse?
20 Why are you selling it?
21 Are the registration papers in your name?
22 Has a child or non-professional rider been riding it?
23 How well does it carry a mild snaffle bit?
24 How does the horse act when loading it in a horse trailer? Any accidents?
25 How is it with hair clippers?
26 What kind of bit do you usually use? (Severe bits are red flags.)
27 How is the horse in a wash rack?
28 How is it to tie?
29 Do any other vices, health problems, or training issues exist?
30 Will you make sure not to lunge or exercise the horse on the day I come to try it? (Tired horses are well-behaved horses.)

one horse kicking another in a fight for top ranking.

RED RIBBONS
If a horse has a red ribbon tied in its tail, it serves as a warning to other riders that the horse is a kicker (kicks other horses).

Blacksmiths

+ Blacksmiths are also known as farriers or horseshoers.

+ The word farrier is derived from the Latin word for iron worker.

+ Men and women can be farriers, but the work is hard on the back and joints, and there is the danger of getting kicked or stomped.

+ A farrier is considered an artist and a scientist. The horse's feet need to be trimmed to the correct angle, size, and shape with proper shoe placement for particular purposes.

+ Some farriers do cold shoeing, conforming the hoof to the shoe; and some do hot shoeing, custom-molding the shoe to the trimmed hoof.

+ Horseshoe nails are driven into the lower part of the hoof that has no feeling, just like the top portion of a human's fingernail.

A farrier heating a horseshoe so that it can be molded to the horse's hoof.

Counting the Years

"RISING 6" MEANS THE HORSE IS CLOSER TO 6 YEARS OF AGE, RATHER THAN 5. "SIX OFF" MEANS CLOSER TO 6 THAN 7 YEARS OF AGE.

🐎 Horse Population

Census surveys conducted in 2006–7 by various major equine organizations revealed a thriving world horse population of over 58 million, with current reports closer to 75 million. On the map below are countries with horse populations over 1 million.

UNITED STATES
over 9 million

KAZAKHSTAN
over 1 million

RUSSIAN FEDERATION
over 1 million

MONGOLIA
over 2 million

BRAZIL
nearly 6 million

CHINA
over 7 million

MEXICO
over 6 million

COLUMBIA
over 2 million

ARGENTINA
nearly 4 million

ETHIOPIA
nearly 2 million

Bran is used as a laxative.

HORSE LAXATIVES

✳ A small amount of bran mash, soaked in warm water, is used by many horsemen to aid in keeping a horse regular. Always seek professional advice as to when, and how much, to use.

✳ When a horse has an impaction (stuck food in the intestines), a veterinarian may oil the horse by running a tube down the nose to the stomach and pumping in mineral oil.

Note: *Surveys indicate that there may be less than 20 horses in Guam, less than 30 in Grenada, and zero horses in Rwanda and Saint Helena.*

Three Eyelids

Horses have a third eyelid, which is a nictitating membrane that originates from the inside corner of the eye and closes horizontally to protect the eye while grazing.

Natural Curiosity

Horses are naturally curious animals and tend to
be investigative of objects in their domain. Being
grazers, they do most of their investigating with their
mouths. Horses tend to copy the behavior of other
horses in the herd. Occasionally, this can make
them appear to be collaborating on a project,
such as moving a log, but more than
likely they are just bored and wanting
to experience some enjoyment.

The brown horse appears to
come and help the gray horse
to move the log.

BUGGY BOOM

Founded in the late 19th century in the U.S.,
Sears, Roebuck & Co. quickly flourished as a
mail-order company, selling everything from
watches and jewelry to clothes and furniture.
Supposedly, in 1897, the company claimed
to be selling a one-horse buggy—a light, one-
horse carriage—every 10 minutes from their
mail-order catalog.

HORSEY TERMS
• Horseplay (boisterous play)
• Horsing around (boisterous play)
• Horselaugh (loud laugh)
• Horseless carriage (car)
• Iron horse (train)
• Nightmare (bad dream)
• Horse sense (common sense)
• Horsepower (unit of power)
• Wild goose chase (Irish
  equestrian sport)
• Dark horse (long shot)
• Workhorse (hard worker)
• Horsefeathers (nonsense)

Pintos

+ There are two different Pinto color patterns:
  1) The tobiano appears to be white with large spots of color.
  2) The overo appears to be a colored horse with jagged white markings on the body. Many overos have bald (all-white) faces.

+ Some Pintos have a medicine hat, which means they have dark ears and poll (top of the head), surrounded by white. They appear to be wearing a dark cap.

+ Pinto is a common surname in Portugal, Italy, and Spain.

+ The pinto bean is mottled in its coloring.

+ The Ford Pinto was a popular economy car in the 1970s.

+ A famous Pinto was Little Joe Cartwright's horse on the *Bonanza* television series, called Cochise.

Pinto beans

An overo Pinto—white markings on a colored body—with a white face.

HORSES DOWN UNDER
Historical records indicate that horses were not introduced into Australia until 1788.

Horses enjoy splashing in mud.

RAIN ROT

Mud that dries on a horse can clog pores, damage hair follicles, and leave temporary bald spots called rain rot.

DO HORSES GET HICCUPS?

* *Horses can hiccup, which is a phenomenon also known as thumps.*

* *Whereas in humans a hiccup is heard in the throat, a horse's hiccup starts near the diaphragm and creates an audible thump sound in the chest area, sometimes accompanied by a rhythmic jerk in the flank area.*

* *Hiccups are reported more often in endurance horses and racehorses that run for prolonged periods of time. They are also known to be caused by an electrolyte imbalance, sometimes in conjunction with colic or diarrhea.*

Pegasus constellation

1914 children's book illustration of Bellerophon riding Pegasus.

The Winged Horse

Pegasus was the winged horse of Greek mythology, supposedly born of the snake-haired monster, Medusa. Pegasus had many adventures, including helping the hero Bellerophon in his fight against the Amazons (a tribe of all-female warriors) and the Chimera (monstrous creatures made from parts of various animals). After slaying the Chimera, Bellerophon tried to ride Pegasus to the top of Mount Olympus to join the gods, but Zeus, the king of the gods, sent a gadfly to sting Pegasus and thereby cause Bellerophon to fall. Granted sanctuary on the gods' mountain, Pegasus carried thunderbolts for Zeus and was ridden by Eos, the goddess of dawn. Zeus eventually transformed Pegasus into a constellation in the heavens. Pegasus became known as the horse of poets.

Horses usually know their way home.

S   N

Homing Horses

✳ If a horse gets loose, herd instincts may keep it from running too far away from other horses.

✳ When a trail rider falls off a horse, the horse, with its keen sense of direction, is apt to run back home.

I'M LOSING MY HAIR

★ Horses start shedding their coats as the days (photoperiods) get longer. The long hairs can be brushed out over a period of about a month, leaving a short, smooth, shiny coat.

★ Show horses can be tricked into keeping a year-round short and shiny coat, by having them wear an insulated horse blanket and staying inside a warm box stall with a light set to a timer. The light is kept on for a few hours after the sun sets, making the daylight hours appear long. If the light goes off by accident, or the horse gets chilled, a winter coat may start growing in an odd manner, with sporadic growth of long, coarse hairs that are often called elephant hairs.

Horses can be tricked into keeping a shiny summer coat.

HORSEY PHRASES

• "That's a horse of a different color." (odd, different)

• "You're beating a dead horse." (doing something pointless)

• "Don't put the cart before the horse." (out of order, backward)

• "She's chomping on the bit." (eager, excited, anxious)

• "He's rearing to go." (eager, excited, anxious)

• "He works like a horse." (hard worker)

• "Get off your high horse." (stop being arrogant, pious)

• "She's stubborn as a mule." (rebellious, stubborn)

• "They're off and running." (great start)

• "The old gray mare ain't what she used to be." (aging, not as productive)

• "I'm so hungry, I could eat a horse." (really hungry)

• "Happy trails." (best wishes)

• "She's long in the tooth." (old)

• "What are the odds?" (surprising, unbelievable)

• "Get back on that horse." (persistence, overcoming)

• "She's kicking up her heels." (frisky, energetic)

• "He's back in the saddle again." (persistence, overcoming)

• "He's feeling his oats." (frisky, energetic)

Horse Categories

Horse breeds fall into four categories: ponies, coldbloods, hotbloods, and warmbloods.

A coldblood Belgian Draft Horse with farmyard friends.

PONIES

Pony breeds are defined as being under 14.2 hands— under 58 inches (147 cm). Many pony breeds have developed in the wild, and this has led to a natural hardiness that is not found in most horse breeds.

The sturdy Haflinger pony is noted for liking people.

COLDBLOODS

Usually refers to the large, bulky, draft horse breeds, such as the Shire, Clydesdale, and Belgian. These horses are known to be docile and insensitive, and are often called gentle giants.

The Arabian is a lively hotblood.

HOTBLOODS

Usually refers to Arabians, Thoroughbreds, and other horses of oriental origin. These horses are known to be energetic and sensitive, or hot.

WARMBLOODS

Originally a cross between a hotblood and a coldblood, resulting in a trainable, athletic horse, often used as a sport horse for dressage, jumping, eventing, and so on. European breeders have warmblood registries that represent particular lineage, such as Hanoverian, Holsteiner, Oldenburg, Trakehner, Dutch Warmblood, and Swedish Warmblood. These European horses are highly sought after in other countries, resulting in a large exportation market.

Warmbloods are used as sport horses.

Horses enjoy cereal bars.

Eat Your Cereal

✳ Horses that are breeding, pregnant, lactating (nursing), working hard, or growing usually need more nutrients beyond roughage (hay/grass), in the form of cereal grains (concentrates).

✳ Popular grains (the seeds of cereal plants) include oats, corn, barley, bran, wheat, milo, rye, and rice, often mixed in various combinations.

✳ Oats are one of the most popular grains. Corn provides two times the energy of oats, but it is often associated with an increase in the risk of cecal acidosis, resulting in colic, laminitis, and founder.

✳ Grains are usually fed as an energy source. Hence the saying, "He is feeling his oats."

✳ Grains are often the primary ingredient of horse cookies and cereal bars.

✳ **Helpful Hint:** Lock up all hay and grain—horses that get loose will eat to the point of getting deathly ill.

Cereal grains are an important source of energy for horses.

STAYING AT THE RITZ

Some horse owners build horse barns with stalls nice enough to house humans.

☆ Stalls usually have an automatic watering fountain in the corner.

☆ The standard size for a box stall is 12 x 12 feet (3.6 x 3.6 m). Bigger ones are needed for foaling mares, and larger horses.

☆ Stalls often have rubber matting on the floor covered by about 8–12 inches (20–30 cm) of bedding.

☆ Horse bedding usually consists of sawdust or straw, but new products are being made with shredded paper and other recyclable materials.

☆ Stalls are usually sifted through once or twice a day, removing manure and wet spots. This is called mucking or mucking out.

☆ Most horses do not feel imprisoned in a stall, as a human would.

☆ Pens that are 12 x 24 feet (3.6 x 7.3 m) or larger are usually called paddocks or corrals. A larger area would be called a pasture.

☆ **Tip:** Be careful about turning out horses that do not know each other into a corral or pasture. Often, they will argue to establish an order of hierarchy.

Stall Myth
If a horse comes out of its stall with the front right foot first, it is supposedly a sign of good luck, and vice versa.

Children and the Horse Bug

✦ Some kids get the horse bug (a feverish desire to be around horses), which has obvious symptoms. They will talk a lot about horses, play with horse toys, pretend to be a horse, write stories about horses, and beg to ride horses. When they do ride, they are usually excited about going back to ride again.

✦ It is true that the horse bug is contagious, and many children will acquire the passion through exposure. However, just like those parents who encourage children to play the piano to no avail, some children will never develop an interest in horses. This is a sad thing for lifelong horsemen who want their own children to follow in their footsteps.

C'est Français

DRESSAGE IS A FRENCH WORD THAT MEANS TRAINING.

A young girl takes her Shetland Pony for a walk.

Hockey on Horseback

Polo, often referred to as hockey on horseback, is believed to have originated in Persia (modern-day Iran) over 2,500 years ago. One of the oldest recorded team sports, it became known as the game of kings.

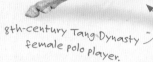

8th-century Tang Dynasty female polo player.

+ The sport spread to various countries, including England in 1869, and shortly thereafter to America. It became especially popular in Argentina, with the country ranked as the polo world champion uninterrupted since 1949.

+ Eight horses (four per team) traveling in all directions at 30 miles per hour (48 kph), and a flying 4½-ounce (125-g) wooden or plastic ball, make this a sport for the hardy.

+ A chukka is the 7–7½-minute play period. Usually, 4–8 chukkas are played per game.

+ The outdoor polo field is the largest field for sporting events at 300 x 160 yards (274 x 146 m).

+ The indoor version of the game is called arena polo, and snow polo is another modern variant.

+ Polo was at times an Olympic event, until 1936.

A polo match in Barbados.

WHITE FEET INFERIOR?

Most horses have dark-colored feet. A horse with a white leg marking can have a white hoof. Some horsemen believe that white hooves tend to be less hardy, subject to chipping.

Thin-skinned

THICKNESS OF SKIN VARIES IN SOME BREEDS, MAKING SOME HORSES MORE REACTIVE AND SENSITIVE TO TOUCH. ARABIANS AND THOROUGHBREDS ARE KNOWN TO BE THIN-SKINNED.

PIG EYES

A horse with small eyes is said to be pig-eyed. Some horsemen avoid purchasing such horses, in the belief that they tend to be spookier and less trainable.

Salt blocks provide horses with extra sodium and sometimes minerals.

small eyes are known as pig eyes.

SALT HOGS

Many horse owners provide salt blocks (some with a small percentage of added minerals) for their horses to lick. Some horses get carried away with this, and can consume a block (intended for a few months) in a matter of days.

★ A white salt block usually only contains salt.

★ A blue salt block usually has the addition of cobalt and iodine.

★ A red salt block usually has iodine added.

★ A brown salt block usually contains additional minerals.

Warning: Always read the label to make sure of the percentages of minerals. Some blocks have extremely high amounts, with potential for problems.

 # Gestation

★ The gestation (pregnancy) period of a mare is normally 11 months (approximately 340 days).

★ Foals born before 320 days' gestation are considered premature, and often have life-threatening respiratory problems.

★ Some mares have reported gestation periods exceeding one year. Claims of up to 417 days exist.

mares are pregnant for almost a year—or even longer.

Horse Gaits

Most horses have four natural gaits.

❶ *Walk: A four-beat gait, with each foot stepping separately.*

❷ *Trot (English) or jog (western):*
A two-beat gait, with diagonal pairs of legs forming one beat.

❸ *Canter (English) or lope (western):*
A three-beat gait—beat one is either of the hindlegs; beat two is the remaining hindleg and diagonal foreleg together; beat three is the remaining foreleg.

❹ *Gallop: A four-beat run, with each foot stepping separately.*

LEADS

❋ When a horse canters (English) or lopes (western), it is in a three-beat gait.

❋ If the horse is traveling to the right, it should be on the right lead, which means its right foreleg will be the last leg to hit the ground, appearing as if the horse is leading with its right foreleg.

❋ If the horse is cantering to the left, it should be on the left lead. The last beat will be the left foreleg, looking as if the horse is leading with that leg.

❋ If the horse is on the incorrect lead on a circle, the horse may feel rough and off-balance.

STRIPES ARE IN

It is not uncommon for gray, spotted, or patterned colored horses, such as the Appaloosa or Pony of the Americas, to have alternating dark and white striped hooves.

CANTER OR LOPE?

In a competition, sometimes English and western riders show in the same class. Should the ring announcer say canter or lope? Sometimes they say cantalope.

Water Horses

Hippopotamus, in many languages, is translated as water horse or river horse.

Rocking horses may date back to medieval times.

WHAT'S IN A NAME?

❋ Some of the most common horse names are Lady, Princess, Lightning, Star, and Lucky.

❋ Purebred horses usually have common barn names as well as registered names. Registered names might include the name of the sire (father), and/or the dam (mother), and/or the breeder.

❋ In Arabians, "ibn" means "son of," and "bint" means "daughter of."

❋ The first successful song for the group America was "A Horse With No Name."

Rocking Horses

+ Rocking horses became popular in the 18th and 19th centuries as toys.

+ Many had real horse hair, and they are now prized collector's items.

+ They evolved into present-day bouncing horses, which are supported on springs so that children can bounce up and down as well as rock.

An old Vietnamese stamp featuring a rocking horse.

Barn Sour

When separated, horses sometimes scream for each other and get agitated. When this happens to a horse leaving the barn, it is said to be barn sour or herd bound.

Glass Eyes

+ When a horse is said to have glass eyes, this does not mean that the eyes are really made of glass. Also known as blue eyes, moon eyes, night eyes, or walleyes, glass eyes are simply eyes that lack color, with a whitish or bluish white iris.

+ Horses with such eyes are known to see just as well as horses with dark eyes.

+ Some horses may have just one glass eye, and one normal-colored brown eye.

+ Some show horses that have lost an eye do have real glass-eye prosthetics.

GIFT HORSE
"Don't look a gift horse in the mouth" is a saying that likely originated from the practice of telling a horse's age by examining the teeth. If someone gives you a horse, be grateful. Looking into its mouth is like checking out a price tag to see what a gift is worth.

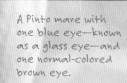

A Pinto mare with one blue eye—known as a glass eye—and one normal-colored brown eye.

Rearing and Bucking Horses

Some horses tend to rear (stand on hindlegs) with a rider as a means of rebellion or playfulness, and others tend to buck (lowering the head and neck and kicking up the hindlegs). Unfortunately (except for rodeo horses), some horses do both equally well.

If a horse bucks, it is considered best to lean back, and pull the reins up to raise the horse's head. It is hard for the horse to buck with its head up.

If a horse rears, it is considered best to lean forward and free up on the rein hold—you do not want to flip the horse backward.

PECOS BILL AND WIDOW MAKER

The mythical cowboy Pecos Bill rode a horse named Widow Maker. When Bill proposed to his girlfriend, Slue-foot Sue, she insisted on riding Bill's horse. The jealous Widow Maker bucked Sue off his back, whereupon Sue bounced up and down for days, even bumping her head on the Moon during a failed attempt by Bill to lasso her. In some versions of the story, Sue eventually recovers but swears off Bill and cowboys in general; in others, Bill shoots her to put her out of her misery. A version of the story is told in the 1948 Disney animated film *Melody Time*. In the Disney story, Sue lands on the Moon, rather than hitting her head on it. Having lost his beloved Sue, Bill goes to live among the coyotes, howling at the Moon in grief. The coyotes howl with him in sympathy—and have done so ever since.

If you ride in a western saddle, it has a wonderful handle called the horn. You may want to grab that horn with one hand to keep your balance on a bucking or rearing horse.

Facial Markings

The size and shape of the facial markings are a useful means of describing and identifying an individual horse, and are recorded on veterinary certificates and other documents in addition to details of the horse's height, sex, color, age, and breed. The size and position of a star should be noted, as should the width of a stripe.

HOW TO BRIGHTEN MARKINGS

❶ *Wash the white marking using a shampoo that contains a bluing agent (human products are fine).*

❷ *Mix cornstarch and water to form a paste.*

❸ *Apply the paste to the wet marking, and let it dry completely.*

❹ *Lightly brush off the top layer of crusty cornstarch to reveal a beautiful bright white marking. Show time!*

BLAZE

IRREGULAR BLAZE

STRIPE

INTERRUPTED STRIPE

SNIP

STRIPE (OR THIN BLAZE) AND SNIP

FAINT STAR

STAR

IRREGULAR STAR

STAR AND STRIPE

LIP MARKING

BALD OR WHITE FACE

Cheetahs are faster, but horses may have greater endurance.

Outrun a Cheetah?

The cheetah is considered to be the fastest of all land animals for a short dash, but belief exists that the horse may have better endurance. Horses are reported to run at top speeds of 43 miles per hour (69 kph), whereas the cheetah is at least 15 miles per hour (24 kph) faster.

Pick debris out of your horse's hooves to prevent lameness.

HOOF PICKIN'

Before AND after riding a horse, riders are encouraged to use a hoof pick to pry out manure and other items, such as glass, rocks, and nails, that can easily lodge in the feet. Failure to remove these items can cause stone bruises and cuts, resulting in lameness.

HORSE TOYS

* A vast array of horse toys are available in tack stores for horses that tend to get bored.
* Most horses enjoy tossing traffic cones, and playing with tethered balls and plastic bottles.

Keep your horse stimulated by giving it toys to play with.

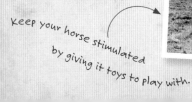

Austrian vaulter Katharina Faltin performing at the 2006 F.E.I. World Equestrian Games in Aachen, Germany.

Vaulting

* Vaulting is referred to as dance and gymnastics on horseback.

* Over 2,000 years ago, Romans would practice their riding education with vaulting exercises.

* Vaulting was demonstrated in the 1920 Olympics under the title of "Artistic Riding."

* Vaulting is an international event at the F.E.I. World Equestrian Games, traditionally dominated by Germany.

That Horse Looks Familiar

Replicas of Greek horse statues abound in hotels, restaurants, and homes throughout the world. The Parthenon, in Athens, an ancient Greek temple dedicated to the goddess Athena, housed horse art that is sometimes referred to as the Parthenon horse. The baroque, muscular, athletic horses have a distinct look that often serves as inspiration for modern-day painters, sculptors, and jewelry makers.

The Parthenon in Athens.

Horses from the marble frieze of the Parthenon.

FIRST AID AT THE STABLES

At your stables, you should have:

+ A first-aid booklet/chart and kit for humans.

+ A first-aid booklet/chart and kit for horses.

+ All emergency numbers posted, including extra veterinarians in case yours is not available.

+ A refrigerator (under security) with drugs to sedate a horse in case of extreme emergency, and ice packs for injuries to horses and riders.

HORSE FIRST-AID KIT

This should include the following basic items:

• Thermometer
• Tweezers
• Scissors
• Knife
• Adhesive tape
• Dose syringes
• Mortar and pestle for pulverizing pills
• Rolls of cotton and gauze
• Clean towels
• Self-stick vet wrap
• Clean standing wraps
• Betadine solution
• Lubricant
• Disinfectant
• Rubbing alcohol
• Liniment
• Antiseptics
• Antibacterial soap
• Epsom salts
• Boric acid powder
• Eye rinse
• Triple antibiotic cream

CALORIES BURNED WHILE RIDING

Below are estimates of calories burned per hour for a 150-pound (68-kg) person:

☆ Saddling, grooming, and general riding for one hour = 238 calories.

☆ Riding at the walk for one hour = 175 calories.

☆ Riding at the trot for one hour = 450 calories (and a lot of pain in the rider's posterior).

☆ Galloping for one hour = 550 calories (and an exhausted, lame horse).

☆ So how does this compare to other activities? Well, high-impact aerobics and moderate bicycling at about 12–14 miles per hour (19–22.5 kph) can each burn approximately 500 calories per hour. General house cleaning can burn about 246 calories per hour, which is similar to general riding.

☆ Riders of smooth-gaited, well-trained horses do not expend as much energy as those who ride young, inexperienced horses or rough, bouncy horses.

☆ Mucking stalls (manure removal) is where you can really burn calories. Many horse owners replace gym memberships with this money-saving aerobic exercise.

Who needs an exercise bike? Riding and caring for a horse will help you keep fit.

Hindi Horses

+ In India, some ancient Vedic religious rituals involved sacrificing horses as a means of ensuring fertility.

+ Dyaus Pita is Hinduism's "Sky Father," who is depicted in art in the form of a black horse or a red bull.

+ Gandharvas are male nature spirits, usually part-human and part-horse, with musical skills.

A colorful fresco in Mandawa, India, depicting erotic figures in the form of a horse.

NIGHT NAVIGATION

Horses have naturally long whiskers that serve as feelers that help the horse to navigate at night.

BOWLEGGED RIDERS

✦ Various writings about Attila and the Huns record the bloodthirsty Huns as masters of horsemanship who were known to be stout in stature, and bowlegged from supposedly spending so much time on their horses.

✦ Zane Grey, best known for his western adventure novels such as *The Man of the Forest* (1920), as well as countless authors throughout the ages, have written about bowlegged horsemen.

An Arabian colt with long whiskers to help it navigate—and a thick baby coat to keep it warm.

Clicker Training

Clicker training is the common term for operant conditioning, where the animal responds to positive consequences and avoids negative ones.

Clicker

Reward

+ In clicker training, the reward is given while a desired behavior is happening, rather than afterward. A little handheld clicker makes a sound that the horse learns to associate with desired behaviors. The click is accompanied by a reward (often a piece of carrot or handful of grain).

+ All training is done in approximations (small increments that are close to the desired behavior, but not perfect).

+ An example of this method would be training a horse to shake hands. The horse is rewarded if it just lifts a foot off the ground. Eventually, the horse works harder to get a delayed reward, lifting the leg higher to get a click and reward.

❶ The trainer touches the horse's nose with the target and clicks at the same time. She then immediately gives the horse a food reward.

❷ Soon, the horse will reach to touch the target wherever it is placed.

EAR PLUGS NEEDED

Horse ears are like mini radar dishes, constantly rotating almost 360 degrees. The horse can hear sounds and pitches that the human ear does not detect. To limit the distractions, some horsemen use ear plugs on their horses when riding in parades or competitions.

Galvayne's groove

Galvayne's groove is just beginning to appear at the top of the incisor of this Norwegian Fjord pony.

Teeth: Birth Certificates

Age can be roughly estimated by looking at the number, size, and shape of a horse's teeth. Another useful marker is Galvayne's groove, which is a dark groove on the upper corner incisor teeth.

+ Galvayne's groove appears at around age ten at the top and middle of the upper corner incisors.

+ By age 15, the groove proceeds halfway down the teeth.

+ By age 20, it completely goes down the teeth and starts to disappear from the top.

+ By age 25, the groove disappears from the top half of the teeth, and remains visible on the bottom half.

+ By age 30, the groove is usually gone.

THERE'S A FROG IN THE FOOT

✤ Horses have a V-shaped projection called a frog on the sole of the hoof, in the middle, toward the heel.

✤ It is believed to act as a shock absorber, relieving concussion on hard surfaces.

✤ When the horse steps down, the frog hits the ground and helps push blood back up the leg, aiding in circulation.

The V-shaped frog may act as a shock absorber.

Lady Godiva

Countless songs, movies, operas, and books have been written about the legendary Lady Godiva, who rode naked, covered only by her long hair, through the streets of Coventry in England around the mid-11th century. There are various versions of Godiva's legendary ride. A popular version of the story is that her husband imposed heavy tax tolls on the people of Coventry, and she pitied them. She appealed to her husband many times, and he eventually made a sarcastic deal that if she agreed to ride through the streets naked, he would abolish the tolls. She took him up on the offer, which had the stipulation that the townspeople were to shut their windows and not look. Part of the legend is that a man named Tom disobeyed, peeked at her, and was struck blind, resulting in the term "Peeping Tom."

Lady Godiva rode a horse naked so that her husband would abolish harsh taxes.

A BALANCED BACK

It is widely believed that a horse's back should be approximately one-third of the length of its body for good balance and movement, but other parts need to be proportionate as well.

⅓ ⅓ ⅓

These proportions of overall body length are considered good conformation.

Equinophobia is the fear of horses.

WOW, THAT HORSE HAS CHROME!

A horse that has a lot of white on its legs is sometimes said to have a lot of chrome.

Thoroughbreds dominate racing, but also compete in show jumping, eventing, and dressage.

THE TRIPLE CROWN

The Triple Crown consists of three races for three-year-old Thoroughbreds that must be won in succession. There are Triple Crown events in many countries around the world; winning the Triple Crown is a rare achievement in all of them.

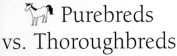 Purebreds vs. Thoroughbreds

Question: All Thoroughbreds are purebreds, but not all purebreds are Thoroughbreds. How can that be?

Answer: A purebred is a horse that is derived from a single breed line. Thoroughbreds are a specific pure breed of horse registered with a recognized breed registry. Other breeds, such as the Arabian, Morgan, Welsh, and Standardbred, are also purebreds.

The Thoroughbred oozes quality, elegance, and superior breeding.

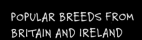

THE THOROUGHBRED

Descended from Arabian stock, the Thoroughbred can rightly be said to be the most important modern breed of horse. Its development over the last 250 years has been phenomenal. It was initially bred entirely for racing for the amusement of the British royalty, aristocracy, and gentry, but the popularity of the sport among the general public and the lure of gambling led to the spread of Thoroughbred racing and breeding to every continent of the world. The Thoroughbred can be highly strung and requires very sensitive, skilled handling, but the horse is also noted for its courage, toughness, and elegance.

Thoroughbred Taboos

THE THOROUGHBRED INDUSTRY DOES NOT ALLOW REGISTERED THOROUGHBREDS TO BE BRED BY MEANS OF ARTIFICIAL INSEMINATION OR EMBRYO TRANSFERS. IT IS BELIEVED THAT THESE STRICT CONTROLS LESSEN THE CHANCE OF MISTAKES OR MISUSE OF GENETIC MATERIAL.

POPULAR BREEDS FROM BRITAIN AND IRELAND

- Anglo-Arabian
- Cleveland Bay
- Clydesdale
- Connemara
- Dales Pony
- Dartmoor Pony
- Exmoor Pony
- Fell Pony
- Hackney
- Highland Pony
- Irish Draught
- New Forest
- Shetland Pony
- Shire Horse
- Suffolk Punch
- Thoroughbred
- Welsh Cob
- Welsh Mountain Pony
- Welsh Pony

Value of Owning a Horse

Owning a horse can be expensive when paying for monthly board, horseshoes, vet care, training, lessons, competitions, and so on. The returns, however, are priceless, especially for children and adolescents. Here are a few of the benefits:

+ Many a parent will readily attest to how horses kept their child occupied and out of trouble, especially during the often difficult teen years.

+ Riding and caring for horses require the formation of a relationship built on mutual respect and trust. Therapeutic riding centers capitalize on this outlet to teach relationship skills through horses.

+ Character building is a natural part of horse ownership, teaching responsibility, punctuality, sportsmanship, frugality, patience, commitment, confidence, and self-esteem.

+ Horses can be a source of mental rejuvenation and stress-relief for the owner— a chance to go to a place very different from typical daily activities.

BUYING TIPS

+ *Search for a well-recommended horse trainer who can select a horse that matches your:*
  1) temperament
  2) size
  3) riding skills
  4) future riding goals
  5) pocketbook

+ *Have a veterinarian inspect the horse, and possibly x-ray the legs.*

+ *Get everything in writing.*

Riding and caring for a horse are character-building experiences.

MISTY OF CHINCOTEAGUE

The 1961 film *Misty* was based on Marguerite Henry's children's book about a real life wild-herd pony, Misty, and a family on the coastal island of Chincoteague, near Maryland in the U.S. After the film, the Ash Wednesday storm of 1962 damaged the island. During the storm, Misty was brought into the owner's home, where she gave birth to a foal named Stormy that became inspiration for another children's book. Misty died in 1972, and was preserved via taxidermy for visitors to view when they come in the summers for the pony penning, when the wild pony herd of Chincoteague crosses the Assateague Channel. Money is raised at this event to preserve the wild pony herd.

A wild pony on the salt water flats of the Assateague Channel.

Deworming

VETERINARIANS CAN TREAT A HORSE FOR WORMS BY PUMPING A DEWORMING AGENT THROUGH A TUBE, DOWN THE HORSE'S NOSE, AND INTO THE STOMACH. WORMING PRODUCTS ALSO COME IN PILL AND PASTE FORM.

HORSE DOWN!

A horse may lie down for reasons other than sleep:

❋ A horse with colic (stomach ache) will tend to lay down and periodically look at its stomach.

❋ Horses may lay flat out, basking in the sun and soaking up the rays.

❋ Some untrained horses have been known to go down on the ground to get a rider off their back.

❋ If sweaty or wet, most horses will roll in the dirt to get dry, as if using a towel.

❋ **Tip:** After spending an hour bathing your horse, it is wise to keep the horse tied until dry. Otherwise, expect the horse to roll in the dirt.

Horses roll in the dirt to get dry, and also to soak up the sun's rays.

Russian standard bearer, 1812

Model Horses

Breyer, an international model horse company, produces over 5 million models a year. These realistic models are made in the colors and likeness of most horse breeds. Collectors of these horses attend model horse shows, similar to doll shows.

Model of a gray Oldenburg.

THOSE FUNKY ERGOTS AND CHESTNUTS

* Most horses have ergots and chestnuts, which are unusual growths similar in substance to a horn or human fingernail.

* Ergots—tubular growths—are on the back of the fetlocks (the joints that look like ankles), hidden within the hair tuft.

* Chestnuts—circular growths similar to a scar or wart—are found on the insides of the legs, just above the knees on the front legs and below the hocks (the joints that look like knees) on the hindlegs.

* Chestnuts and ergots do grow and build up to the point that a horseshoer may be required to clip them flat. It is sometimes possible to pull them off gradually, layer by layer.

* Evolutionists believe these to be remnants of a digital pad that once formed the toes on prehistoric horses.

At Your Service

* Throughout history, horses have been used for battle, transportation, farming, and ranching.

* Today, horses are primarily used for mounted police work, rescue efforts, transportation (riding and driving), ranch work, recreation, entertainment, racing, competition, and equine-assisted therapy.

* Some Miniature Horses are now being used as seeing-eye horses for the blind.

The Peruvian Paso opposite has a large chestnut on one of its forelegs.

Listen to the Beat

+ The Peruvian Paso horse is judged in competitions while being ridden on a long wooden floorboard (fino board), measuring about 4 x 30 feet (1.2 x 9 m).

+ Judges often shut their eyes and listen to the rhythm of the unique four-beat lateral gait called the paso llano. The judges get satisfaction out of hearing how close together (quick) the footfalls can be. The horses appear as if they are in a hurry, but in reality they are covering very little ground. Breeders of these horses claim that they are the world's smoothest riding horses.

+ Charros (Mexican cowboys) typically ride Quarter Horses and Andalusians (or a cross between the two, called an Azteca). Accompanied by mariachi music, they often hold horse-dancing competitions on a wooden sound board. The horses are given a few minutes to demonstrate movements, such as the piaffe, which is a sort of lively trot on the spot.

The Peruvian Paso's special gait is natural, with very little vertical bounce, making it very comfortable for the rider.

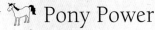

Pony Power

+ Ponies are full-grown, small horses that are 14.2 hands high (hh)—58 inches (147 cm)—or less.

+ Many trainers like to use ponies for children, because there is less distance to fall.

+ Ponies often get a bad rap, being stereotyped as mischievous and hard to train. Keep in mind that pony trainers must be small, and are therefore often children, which may contribute to this belief.

+ Popular pony breeds: Welsh, Shetland, Pony of the Americas, Halflinger, Connemera, and Hackney.

+ The Pony Club is an international organization devoted to educating young riders with ponies.

ARE HORSES PETS?

✤ Many owners consider horses to be pets, and even part of the family. Many people buy birthday and Christmas gifts for their horses.

✤ Laws relating to taxes and waste often categorize horses as livestock or agricultural animals, not as companion animals or pets.

✤ Many argue that horses are service animals that contribute to society beyond use as livestock.

Some Shetland Ponies make good children's mounts, but others are domineering and headstrong.

SMALL BUT STRONG
One Shetland Pony of 9 hands— 36 inches (91 cm)— in height is reported to have carried a 168-pound (76-kg) man a distance of 40 miles (64 km) in one day.

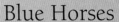

COATS OF ARMS

A pair of rampant horses are used as supporters for the central shield in many coats of arms. The horses symbolize readiness for all events.

Pennsylvania coat of arms.

Blue Horses

+ Perhaps one of the rarest colors of horse is the grulla (pronounced _grew-ya_) or grullo (_grew-o_), also known as the black dun, blue dun, or lobo dun.

+ The coat color is the result of the dun gene on top of a black gene, which produces individual hairs that are a mousy gray, smoky blue, or slate gray color. Grullo horses can vary quite widely, from a distinctive smoky blue to a mousy tan.

+ Often these horses have a dorsal stripe on the back, a dark face, dark ear tips and edging, dark mane and legs, and leg barring (called tiger striping).

+ The Spanish word _grulla_ refers to a slate-gray crane.

Gender Biased?

⋆ _In some cultures, horses are primarily ridden by men, and the horse often represents machismo. In other cultures, such as the U.S., horses are more likely to be owned and ridden by females._

⋆ _Regardless of gender, the most important aspect is the personality and temperament of the rider. Most horses require a rider who is sensitive to their feelings and needs._

⋆ _Riding has more to do with reasoning than brute strength._

⋆ _There are equally talented professional riders of both genders that have attained world-class status in the horse industry. When it comes to bareback bronco riding on the professional rodeo circuit, however, it is a different story._

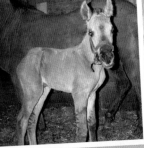

This 1-day-old grulla Quarter Horse filly has a smoky blue-gray tinge to her coat and leg barring.

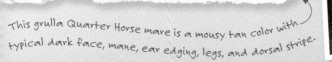

This grulla Quarter Horse mare is a mousy tan color with typical dark face, mane, ear edging, legs, and dorsal stripe.

Famous Horses in Television

Horse .... TV show/TV celebrity rider

Black Beauty .... *The Adventures of Black Beauty*
Buttermilk .... Dale Evan's Buckskin horse in
The Roy Rogers Show
Buck .... Buckskin ridden by Ben Cartwright
in *Bonanza*
Buckshot .... Wild Bill Hickok's horse, appearing
in several TV shows and movies
Bunny .... Laura Ingalls Wilder's horse in
Little House on the Prairie
Candy .... *Shane*
Cochise .... Paint horse ridden by Little Joe in *Bonanza*
Champion .... *Champion the Wonder Horse*
Chub .... Large horse ridden by Hoss in *Bonanza*
Easter Ute .... Appaloosa in *The Virginian*
Edmund .... *Seinfeld*
Mister Ed .... Intelligent talking Palomino in *Mister Ed*
Esquilax .... *The Simpsons*
Fury .... *Fury*
Pokey .... *The Gumby Show*
Pony Puff Princess .... *Dexter's Laboratory*
Princess .... *The Simpsons*
Quick Draw McGraw .... *The Quick Draw McGraw Show*
cartoon series
Rafter .... *Have Gun Will Travel*
Razor .... *The Rifleman*
Rex .... Montie Montana Sr.'s horse in John Wayne
movies and other TV westerns
Scout .... Tonto's horse in *The Lone Ranger*
Skyrocket .... Mickey Mouse Club's *Spin and Marty*
Silver .... Title character's horse in *The Lone Ranger*
Whirleygig .... *I Love Lucy*
White Flash .... Tex Ritter's horse in various TV westerns
Tony .... Tom Mix's horse in various TV westerns
Topper .... Hopalong Cassidy's horse in various
TV westerns
Tornado .... Zorro's horse in the *Zorro* series and movies
Trigger .... Roy Rogers' horse in *The Roy Rogers Show*

NO SILENT MOVIES FOR THESE STARS

Mister Ed (a Palomino Saddlebred) and Francis the Mule were both media stars who were known for their ability to talk in human form. They were both trained by the same professional trainer; they both won PATSY awards (animal Oscars); and they both had musical records.

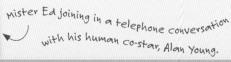

Mister Ed joining in a telephone conversation with his human co-star, Alan Young.

Palominos

+ A Palomino is a yellowish color, light or dark, with a white mane and tail. The color is caused by a dilution gene on a red (chestnut) base coat.

+ A golden Palomino is the color of a gold coin. A dark Palomino is called a chocolate Palomino. A horse that appears almost white, with a tint of yellow, is known as a Cremello.

+ Black or dark hairs mixed within the coat, mane, or tail are usually considered a fault.

+ Famous Palominos include Mister Ed and Roy Rogers' horse Trigger. A taxidermist preserved Trigger to put on display at the Roy Rogers Museum.

+ Singer Bruce Springsteen wrote a song entitled "Silver Palomino."

Roy Rogers with his Palomino pal, Trigger.

A scene from "Bonanza," with (from left to right) Hoss riding Chub, Ben Cartwright riding Buck, and Little Joe riding Cochise.

RETIRED TELEVISION STAR

Buck, the famous Buckskin ridden by Lorne Greene in the *Bonanza* television series, was reportedly purchased by the actor when the show was canceled in 1972. Greene graciously donated the horse to the Fran Joswick Therapeutic Riding Center in California. There, Buck lived a long life, dying at the incredible age of 45, having spent many years of his life as a mount for children with disabilities.

Famous Leaders and Their Horses

**Throughout history, horses have carried many famous leaders into battle
and on momentous journeys. Here are a few of them:**

Mosaic of Alexander
the Great from
Pompeii, Italy.

Portrait of Lü Bu
from a Qing Dynasty
manuscript.

Horse: **Bucephalus**
Leader: **Alexander the Great**
(356–323 B.C.), ancient Greek king
of Macedon

Horse: **Red Hare**
Leader: **Lü Bu** (died A.D. 199), Chinese
military leader and master horseback
rider known as the "Flying General,"
whose story is told in the 14th-century
historical novel *Romance of the Three
Kingdoms* by Luo Guanzhong

Horse: **Babieca**
Leader: **El Cid** (c.1044–99),
Castilian nobleman

Horse: **Blanc Sanglier (White Boar)**
Leader: **Richard III** (1452–85), king
of England

Horse: **Streiff**
Leader: **Gustavus Adolphus**
(1594–1632), Swedish king and
renowned military tactician who
led his country to great success in
the Thirty Years' War

"El Cid" means
"The Lord" or
"Master of
Military Arts."

17th-century
painting of
Gustavus Adolphus.

1911 illustration of George Washington.

HORSE MASTER

The ancient Greek physician Hippocrates was the inspiration for the Hippocratic oath that still serves as the foundation for good medical ethics. His name actually means horse master.

Horses: **Blueskin, Magnolia, (Old) Nelson & Roger Leo**
Leader: **George Washington** (1732–99), commander-in-chief of the revolutionary army against the British and first president of the United States

Horse: **Marengo**
Leader: **Napoleon** (1769–1821), ruler of France after the French Revolution

Horse: **Copenhagen**
Leader: **Duke of Wellington** (1769–1852), commander of Anglo-allied forces in the defeat of Napoleon at Waterloo in 1815

Horse: **Cincinnati**
Leader: **Ulysses S. Grant** (1822–85), Union general in the American Civil War and 18th president of the United States

Napoleon at the Battle of Austerlitz, 1805.

Horse Heads

Different breeds tend to have different standards for what is considered a good head. The extremes are:

✦ The concave head of the Arabian, with its tea-cupped muzzle.

✦ The convex head of some Baroque breeds, such as the Lusitano and Lipizzaner, with a roman nose.

Two young Arabians with tea-cupped muzzles.

A Head in the Bed

IN THE 1972 FILM *THE GODFATHER*, ONE CHARACTER WAKES UP TO FIND THE HEAD OF HIS PRIZED BREEDING STALLION IN THE BED WITH HIM, AS RETALIATION FOR DISPLEASING THE GODFATHER. A FAKE HEAD WAS USED IN REHEARSALS, BUT A REAL HEAD FROM A DOG-FOOD FACTORY WAS USED IN THE FINAL SCENE.

An old Baroque horse with a classic roman nose.

GENDERS, AGES, AND BREEDING TERMS

Foal .... Baby of either gender
Filly .... Baby female, up to four years of age
Colt .... Baby male, up to four years of age
Mare .... Female, four years or older
Broodmare .... Female used for breeding
Dam .... Mother of a foal
Stallion .... Male, four years or older
Stud .... Another name for a stallion or the name for a breeding establishment
Sire .... Father of a foal
Gelding .... Castrated male
Cryptorchid ..... Stallion with testicles not descended
Monorchid .... Stallion with one testicle not descended

Good-quality stabling is essential for all horses at all ages.

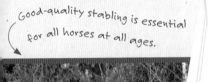

 Horses in Retirement Homes

Profit and non-profit facilities exist around the world for the retirement of horses that are no longer rideable or useful to their owners. Owners can pay for a luxurious retirement facility to take full care of their elderly horses, often placing them with other horses in lush pastures to enjoy their final days. Rescue retirement facilities help horses that are abused, neglected, or headed for the slaughterhouse. Funding for these nonprofit organizations usually comes from the generous donations of horse lovers.

PUT SIGNS ON THE WALL

Here are some of the primary terms that sum up the philosophy and goals of classical dressage (training):

- Obedience
- Relaxation
- Rhythm
- Suppleness
- Swinging motion (also called schwung)
- Contact
- Throughness (flow of energy)
- Straightness
- Impulsion
- Collection
- Balance
- Self-carriage

A rider and horse performing an extended trot during an advanced dressage test.

THAT TIME OF THE MONTH

✤ Females can come into heat (estrus) as early as their yearling year (between one and two years old).

✤ Most females are not bred until they are fully grown (at three or four years of age).

✤ The estrous cycle takes place about every 21 days, with a period of 5–7 days when the mare is receptive to a stallion. The last 24–48 hours of this receptive period is when the mare usually ovulates.

✤ Most horses will only cycle in the spring and summer when the light of day (photoperiod) is longer. This avoids foals being born in the cold of winter.

Painless Posting

✦ Posting or rising is the up-and-down motion of a rider that is in sync with the two beats of a horse's trot—the rider rises out of the saddle on the first beat, and sits down on the saddle on the second beat. Posting allows the rider to avoid absorbing the impact of a rough, bouncy trot.

✦ Western and upper-level dressage riders usually stay seated in the saddle when at a trot, known as sitting the trot. This allows the rider to use the seat to influence the horse, thereby giving the rider more control, but it can be tiring for the rider because of the impact of the trot. Some western riders post in a western saddle when the horse accelerates into a faster, bouncier trot.

🐎 Appaloosas

These colorful horses are not considered a color breed (such as Palomino, Pinto, and Buckskin), but are instead regarded as a definite breed (specific horse heritage) with a color preference.

✦ Appaloosas are cited in ancient European and Asian art. They were brought to the Americas and developed by the Nez Perce people, near the Palouse River in the northwestern United States—hence the name, Appaloosa.

✦ The three main spotted patterns of an Appaloosa are:
1) Blanket pattern: A dark base coat with a white blanket marking over the hindquarters. Base-color spots are often on the white blanket.
2) Leopard pattern: Lots of dark base-color spots all over a white coat.
3) Snowflake pattern: A dark base-color horse with lots of white spots.

ANCIENT HERITGAGE

Spotted and mottled horses were prized among ancient civilizations. Cro-Magnon man (living 10–40,000 years ago) was familiar with spotted horses and left cave drawings of them.

Sclera (white) around the eye.

Base color with a spotted pattern (here, leopard pattern).

Mottled (freckled) skin around the eyes and muzzle.

Striped colored hooves.

 Rodeos

Rodeos originated in the United States as an extension of the day-to-day lives of the pioneer cowboys. Catching cattle for branding, and riding young bucking horses, naturally progressed into competitions between the cowboys.

* Today, most rodeos hold seven events, including bareback bronco riding, saddle bronco riding, bull riding, steer wrestling, calf roping, team roping, and cowgirls' barrel racing.

* A typical unbroken horse costs about $1,000 (£500). A top-ranked bucking horse or bull can be worth over $100,000 (£50,000).

* The word rodeo comes from the Spanish *rodear*, which means to encircle or surround, as cowboys do with cattle. The actual term rodeo was first given to cowboy exhibitions in 1916.

* Animal rights activists are vocal critics of rodeos, claiming that rodeos cause physical and mental distress to the animals involved.

* Rodeos originally held wagon races and marksmanship contests, in addition to the traditional events.

A cowboy closes in on his prey.

"It Came Straight from the Horse's Mouth"

THIS PHRASE IS RUMORED TO HAVE ITS ORIGINS ON THE RACECOURSE—THE MOST RELIABLE TIP WAS SAID TO COME NOT FROM THE BOOKKEEPER, BUT STRAIGHT FROM THE HORSE'S MOUTH.

Fantastic! These guys will believe anything I tell them.

Ears That Talk

A horse's ears can tell you what it is thinking.

✳ If the ears are pricked forward, the horse is concerned or curious about something it sees.

✳ If the ears are relaxed in a neutral position, there is a good chance that the horse is at peace.

✳ If the ears are slightly back, the horse may be expressing some anger. This is a warning.

✳ If the ears are laid flat back, the horse is extremely mad. Watch out!

✳ When riding, it is not uncommon for one ear to be focused back toward the rider as the horse listens to commands, while the other ear is directed toward sounds in front.

Ears forward

Ears back

Ears relaxed

Chaps help prevent soreness on long rides.

HORSE POOP: THE FACTS

✚ A horse produces 33–50 pounds (15–23 kg) of feces per day.

✚ If a horse is kept in confined quarters, the owner must muck out up to 8 tons of waste per year.

✚ Fresh horse feces can stink a bit, but many people actually favor the unique smell of dried horse manure.

✚ Three-quarters of fresh horse poop is water and the last portion is dead bacteria, undigested fiber, fats, dead cells, and phosphates.

✚ Horse feces are usually green if green roughages are eaten. Light-colored hay produces yellowish feces.

✚ Horse manure is a clean, natural product used by landscapers and farmers as topsoil and fertilizer. Special horse-manure composting bins and products are on the market.

Dried horse manure is great for growing roses.

SHAPS, NOT CHAPS

Chaps, short for chaparejos (*shap-ar-EH-hos*), is pronounced "shaps" by most horsemen. These leather britches, or wraparound leggings, were an important cowboy accessory, worn to prevent injury to the legs while chasing cattle.

A beautiful mule.

HORSE CROSSES

- A female horse crossed with a male donkey (jack) = a mule (usually sterile).
- A male horse crossed with a female donkey (jenny) = a hinny (usually sterile).
- A horse crossed with a zebra = a zorse.
- A donkey crossed with a zebra = a zedonk or zonkey.
- So, what is a burro? It is a donkey in the wild.

A Morgan mare, classed as a light horse.

Hippotherapy

★ A major international movement in the horse industry is equine-assisted therapy. Horses, therapeutic riding instructors, and professional therapists work together to benefit the lives of people with physical and mental disabilities. The term hippotherapy means treatment with the help of the horse.

★ In the equine-assisted therapy movement, there are three popular teaching methods: riding, driving, and vaulting. Instructors earn certification for these techniques through various organizations.

Light Horses

LIGHT HORSES ARE HORSES THAT ARE NOT DRAFT (HEAVY) HORSES. EXAMPLES ARE THE ARABIAN, MORGAN, ANDALUSIAN, SADDLEBRED, AND THOROUGHBRED.

An old horse-drawn hearse.

Horses in Mourning

★ In the era of Genghis Khan of the Mongolian Empire, horses were sacrificed to be used by fallen warriors in the hereafter.

★ Primitive northern European beliefs incorporated riderless horses into funerals to signify the need for the fallen warrior to ride in heaven.

★ In the U.S. military, it is tradition to have a riderless horse wearing ornamental tack (called a caparisoned horse) follow the casket of the nation's president (the military's commander-in-chief), or any army or marine corps officer of high status. Riding boots are placed in the stirrups backward to symbolize that the deceased person will never ride again.

Horses at Weddings

✤ It is not uncommon for diehard horse enthusiasts to get married on horseback, uniting husband and wife through their favorite pastime, horses.

✤ Take note. Such a meaningful display of affection can go awry. Many a bride has been bucked off when the wedding dress, or the strange sight, scares the horse. A loose horse running through the crowd of spectators can ruin the desired effect.

A horse dressed up to pull a wedding carriage.

Gone with the Wind

Reportedly, more than 1,100 horses and mules were used in the filming of "Gone with the Wind" (1939).

Dance Moves

The following movements in classical dressage take many years of training to accomplish. Shortcuts in training often result in gimmicky, tense imitations of the true movements.

An early 20th-century painting by Ludwig Koch showing a horse performing a piaffe.

✦ **The Piaffe:** Think of the piaffe as a lively trot in place (on the spot). It is a highly collected movement, with the horse carrying most of its weight on the hindquarters. The leg joints are extremely flexed, and there is a moment of suspension before diagonal pairs of legs hit the ground. The horse is said to be between the rider's hands and legs.

✦ **The Passage:** Think of the passage as a trot in slow motion. It is a powerful trot where the legs flex high and forward, with a period of suspension in the air.

✦ **The Pirouette:** This motion appears to the uneducated eye as if the horse and rider are just cantering in a small circle. Actually, the horse is on two tracks, revolving on two circles. The front half of the body forms a large circle around the hindquarters, where the outside hindleg makes a smaller circle around a lifting and lowering inside hindleg. The horse should complete the pirouette with equal, rhythmic bounds, following a slight inside bend of the body. When done at the walk, this is called a turn on the haunches.

An Azteca horse beginning a canter pirouette to the right.

CAN HORSES REALLY DANCE?

+ Many horsemen wholeheartedly believe that their mounts, with the training of certain steps and maneuvers, can intentionally dance in synchronization with music. The horse's ability to demonstrate rhythm and style can be felt by the rider, and the keen observer.

+ There are traveling dance horse exhibitions, dinner theaters for dancing horses, competitions for dancing horses, and exhibitions where people dance on the ground with horses.

+ Musical freestyle dressage competitions are the epitome of dance perfection, with correct, classical horsemanship choreographed to movements such as the half-pass, flying changes of lead, pirouette, piaffe, passage, collected and extended gaits, and so on.

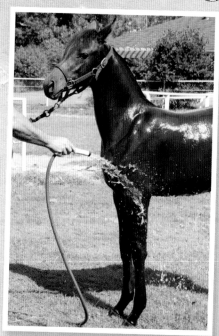

A young Arabian horse gets a cool down.

SPINNING HORSES

In western reining competitions, horses do a tighter, much faster version of the dressage pirouette. Called a spin, it involves keeping the hind pivot foot almost stationary. An old cowboy quote about a fast-spinning horse is:

"He can spin on a dime, and give back change."

🐎 Bathtime

* Bathing once or twice a month with shampoo is probably best. Too much shampoo can deplete the horse's natural oils, making the coat dull and unprotected.

* As often as needed, rinse a sweaty horse with water to remove the salty sweat that can make a horse itchy and sun-bleached.

* Horses must be trained to accept a hose and water. They are naturally fearful of spraying water.

* Manes and tails can be washed with shampoo and conditioner more often, and the tail can be tied up (often put in a tail bag) to keep it clean and unbroken.

* Just like haircare products for people, there are numerous hair products on the market for horses.

Popular Horse Hays

Feed is often selected according to availability within a region. Some of the most popular hays (called roughage or long-stem forage) for horses include the following:

+ Legume hays (non-grass) such as alfalfa, which is higher than most hays in protein and calcium content, but may not be much higher in energy (mega calories per pound or kilogram).

+ Grass hays such as timothy, Sudan grass, smooth brome grass, orchard grass, tall fescue, oat hay, and prairie hay.

+ **Oat Alert:** Oat hay is not commonly used as a horse hay, unless it is in the soft dough, green stage, when it can be used for maintenance of older, non-working horses. White, stemy, grain-free oat hay is merely straw that is only good for stall bedding or insulation.

+ **Alfalfa Alert:** Feeding protein-rich alfalfa hay to young horses is not considered wise. The high calcium content is believed to cause developmental problems in the bones and joints.

Prairie grass

Timothy

Alfalfa

Cowboy Treat
A popular cowboy treat is a stem of alfalfa. You can suck and chew on one for hours.

HAVING A BAD HAIR DAY?

Cowlicks are swirls of hair (tufts of convergent or divergent patterns) that can be found on some horses, usually on the forehead, cheeks, neck, belly, and hips. No amount of styling gel can tame these swirls.

A Clydesdale draft horse with a thick, furry winter coat.

Horse Hair or Fur?

* Definitions of fur are varied, but fur is commonly referred to as the fine, soft, thick, layered coat of a mammal.
* Usually, horses and humans are said to have hair, not fur.
* When horses get their thick winter coats, some people do call them furry.

It's so warm and cozy in my fur coat.

Zebra Stripes
Zebra stripes are like human fingerprints—no two are alike.

The movement of a horse's walk has therapeutic effects that are unequaled by manmade equipment. The walk has three dimensions to the movement: up and down, side to side, and forward and back. This motion benefits a rider's muscular development, coordination, posture, and balance. People who use wheelchairs can ride a horse and experience a sensation that is very similar to the human walk.

Horse Whisperers

In any profession or art, there are individuals who appear to excel above the rest. Some professional trainers are more attuned to the language, emotions, and motivations of horses. These amazing horse communicators are sometimes called horse whisperers.

THE EQUESTRIAN CLASS
The horsemen of the ancient Roman cavalry came from the upper classes of society, because they were able to afford a horse. This indication of wealth meant that it became prestigious to own a horse, although horsemen in the military did also receive a grant for their purchase. Eventually, the term equestrian simply came to indicate that a man was a member of the nobility, and the connection to horses became symbolic.

The equestrian Marcus Aurelius became an emperor of Rome.

WEIGHTY CONSIDERATIONS

An average horse should be able to carry about 25 percent of its body weight.

Category	Horse	Rider
Pony	400 pounds (180 kg)	100 pounds (45 kg)
Small horse	800 pounds (360 kg)	200 pounds (90 kg)
Average-sized horse	1,000 pounds (450 kg)	250 pounds (115 kg)

ZODIAC HORSES

The horse is featured in the Chinese zodiac's 12-year cycle of animals. Chinese astrologists associate certain personality traits—intelligence, independence, and free-spiritedness—with those people born in the year of the horse.

Shire Horses are 16–18 hands high— 64–72 inches (163–183 cm)—or even more.

EXTREME BREED SIZES

The horse breeds that have unusually small sizes often trace to the Falabella breeding program of Argentina. The Shire breed of England is known to produce some of the world's tallest horses.

The Falabella does not exceed 30 inches (76 cm) in height.

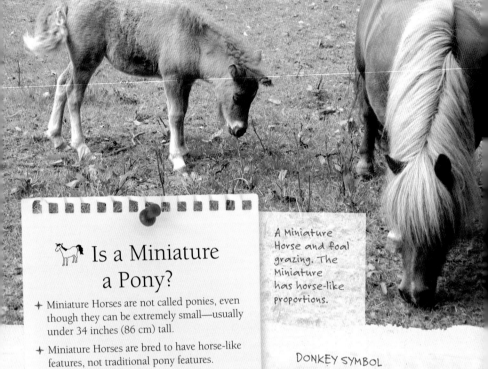

🐴 Is a Miniature a Pony?

+ Miniature Horses are not called ponies, even though they can be extremely small—usually under 34 inches (86 cm) tall.

+ Miniature Horses are bred to have horse-like features, not traditional pony features.

+ Controversy exists over the existence of dwarfism genes in the genetic pool of some breeding programs.

+ Dwarf characteristics (disproportionately large heads and short legs) are considered a fault among most breeders of Miniature Horses.

A Miniature Horse and foal grazing. The Miniature has horse-like proportions.

DONKEY SYMBOL
In Greco-Roman myth, donkeys are known as a symbol of lust.

With these ears, who could resist me?

Mighty Minis

IT IS NOT UNCOMMON FOR A MINIATURE HORSE—UNDER 34 INCHES (86 CM) TALL—TO PULL TWO AVERAGE-SIZED ADULTS IN A CART.

POSITIVE REINFORCERS

❉ Horses respond well to treats such as bits of carrots and apples.

❉ Some horses respond well to soothing, softly spoken words.

❉ Many enjoy getting scratched on the neck, shoulder, face, and other body parts.

❉ The absence of pressure (rider's legs, hands, seat, whips, spurs) is considered a reward.

NEGATIVE REINFORCERS

❉ Whips, crops, and bats are stick-shaped implements that can subtly pressure or persuade a horse to respond a certain way, if used properly.

❉ Spurs on the rider's boots can work in the same way.

❉ A person's voice used loudly, in a firm manner, can also be used as a means of reprimanding.

❉ **Beware:** When whips, spurs, and voice are used harshly or at the wrong time, they can instill fear, resentment, and rebellion.

Racing Colors

✦ Colorful jackets called silks are worn by jockeys to help distinguish horses from each other and improve the likelihood of settling racing disputes. This tradition was started by the English Jockey Club in 1762. Today, owners must register their colors and patterns with the Jockey Club in their region.

✦ Ancient Roman charioteers wore headbands and capes in bright colors for identification—possibly the first time racing colors were used.

Bright colors help spectators to distinguish one competitor from another.

PEEING LIKE A RACEHORSE

Horses urinate close to 2 gallons (7.5 l) of urine per day. The phrase "peeing like a racehorse" is said to be based on the fact that horses excrete such immense volumes of urine, and the image of a racehorse running to the finish line (analogous to someone hurrying to the bathroom).

This Criollo, a South American horse of Spanish descent, has a buzz cut.

Spanish Buzz Cuts

+ P.R.E. Spanish horses (Pura Raza Espanola) have special haircuts with the purpose of showing off conformation, and identifying genders and ages.

+ Colts and fillies under two years of age have their manes, forelocks, and tails completely clipped off.

+ Two-year-old fillies maintain the clipped, short manes, but may grow tail hair starting about 10 inches (25 cm) down the shaved tailbone. Two-year-old colts start growing out their manes and tails.

+ Females three years of age and older keep the clipped, short manes, but may grow longer tail hair below the 8–10 inches (20–25 cm) of shaved tailbone. Males continue to grow long, luxurious manes and tails for the rest of their lives.

EQUITATION

The term equitation refers to the position of the rider (unity and effectiveness of all body parts).

☆ Centuries ago, classic schools of equitation were started in European countries by royal decree. The Royal Riding School in Spain and the Spanish Riding School in Vienna are two such equitation schools that focused on riding as a highly specialized art and science.

☆ Today, riders have their form (equitation) judged in equitation competitions. Equitation classes are held for individual seats (hunt seat, saddle seat, stock seat, and dressage seat).

☆ It is correct to say, "Focus on your equitation." It is considered tacky or slang to tell a rider to "equitate."

☆ Most riding styles (western, hunt, saddle seat, and dressage) consider good equitation to involve proper posture, with a straight line going from the rider's head to the hip and to the heel.

BUYER BEWARE

Many people make the major mistake of buying a horse for an impressive color (black, palomino, pinto), or a luxurious, long, thick mane and tail. Top priorities should be temperament, training, correct conformation, and quality movement (smooth, balanced gaits).

AGE TO CASTRATE

* Controversy exists as to what is the best age to castrate (geld) a male. Some believe that the younger the age of castration, the taller the horse will grow, with less chance of the horse acquiring aggressive behaviors. Others want a horse to remain intact longer so that it will develop more body substance and a shapely, cresty neck. Having a distinctive crest (the topline of the neck) is desirable in some breeds.

* Many breeders feel that only a superior horse should be a stallion for breeding purposes; all others should be gelded, with the belief that most good stallions make great geldings.

* Some cultures have breeds that are seldom castrated. The majority of male Pure Spanish Horses are left intact. Machismo is thought to be one factor in this philosophy.

The Spanish Walk

The Spanish Walk is not used as an element in dressage tests. It is considered by most horsemen to be a trick for exhibition purposes. The horse is trained to walk forward with extreme upper and outer motion of the front legs.

Some breeders believe that the age at which colts are castrated affects their physical development.

An Andalusian stallion performing the Spanish Walk.

OUT LIKE A LIGHTBULB

☆ Horses do not need as much sleep as humans. They tend to need only about 2–4 hours of sleep a day, often in 15–30-minute increments. When horses lie down to sleep, such sleep (REM) is believed to be deeper than a stand-up nap.

☆ Some horses tend to lay down more than others. Feeling safe seems to be a factor. In the wild, horses often stand watch over a horse that is sleeping on the ground.

☆ Most horses will lie flat out, or in a crouched position with their noses (muzzles) propped on the ground.

☆ Some horses that lay down in a box stall (an enclosed stall for a single animal) are prone to getting cast; their legs get stuck against the wall, and they have trouble figuring out how to roll over to get unstuck.

☆ **Tip:** If a horse is kept in a box stall, the stall should be large enough to allow the horse to sprawl out fully. A 12 x 12-foot (3.6 x 3.6-m) stall may not be big enough for all horses.

A mare watching over her foal as it sleeps.

Messy Hair Myth
A horse's tangled mane reveals that pixies and fairies have been riding or playing with the horse.

HOW TO IDENTIFY HORSEPEOPLE

• They click or cluck to their kids when they want them to move.
• Their nice clothes are the ones without horse hair on them.
• They know why there is a yard of string on the end of a horse thermometer.
• They have less wardrobe space than their horse.
• They think nothing of eating a sandwich after mucking out a stall.
• They are the ones stealing all the socks for tail bags.
• They spend hundreds on a show, just to win a piece of ribbon.

Aaron Ralston performing a sliding stop on Smart Paul Olena at the 2006 F.E.I. World Equestrian Games in Aachen, Germany.

OBSTACLE COURSES

An event sometimes held in horse competitions is the trail class, where horses are asked to maneuver over and through intimidating obstacles that might be encountered out on the trails, such as:

✱ Backing with the rider between L-shaped poles.

✱ Walking over a small, narrow bridge.

✱ Side-passing (walking sideways) over a ground pole underneath the horse's belly.

✱ Side-passing to a mailbox and allowing the rider to pick up the mail.

✱ Dragging a bag of cans on a long rope.

✱ Years ago, competitions allowed courses to have live caged animals and activated fire extinguishers, with horses having to walk through water boxes and automobile tires, and over animal hides and rocking bridges. This proved to be a bit unrealistic and dangerous.

Sliding Horses

+ Once confined to the United States, reining is now an international event gaining immense popularity. Wearing western tack, horses work exact patterns similar to ice figure skaters.

+ Patterns include flying lead changes, sliding stops, roll backs, and spins. The sliding stop is amazing. Wearing special shoes, the horses lower their hindquarters and slide to stops that can measure up to 20 feet (6 m) in distance.

+ Choreographed music is sometimes added, known as freestyle reining, as well as events for riders performing without a bridle.

THE ANDALUSIAN

- The modern Andalusian is probably one of the oldest breeds or strains in the world.

- It represents almost exactly the type of horse depicted in Iberian prehistoric cave art.

- Babieca, the mount of Spain's hero, El Cid, was an Andalusian.

- The luxuriant, often wavy, mane and tail of the Andalusian are a feature of the breed and much prized. Manes and tails sweeping the ground are not unknown.

POPULAR BREEDS FROM EUROPE

- Alter Real
- Andalusian
- Ardennes or Ardennais
- Belgian Draft Horse or Brabant
- Breton
- Camargue
- Carthusian
- Danubian
- Dutch Draft
- Dutch Harness Horse
- Dutch Warmblood
- East Bulgarian
- East Friesian
- French Anglo-Arabian
- French Trotter
- Friesian

- Furioso
- Gelderlander
- Gidran
- Haflinger
- Hanoverian
- Holsteiner
- Hucul
- Italian Heavy Draft
- Karacabey
- Kladruber
- Konik
- Lipizzaner
- Lusitano
- Malopolski
- Mecklenburg
- Nonius
- Noriker

- Norman Cob
- Oldenburg
- Percheron
- Pura Raza Espanola (Pure Spanish Horse)
- Rheinlander Pflaz
- Rhineland Heavy Draft
- Salerno
- Schleswig Heavy Draft
- Selle Français
- Shagya Arabian
- Swiss Warmblood
- Trakehner
- Westphalian
- Wielkopolski

IBERIAN HORSES

* Horses that are often called Andalusians can be traced to ancient horses bred along the Iberian coast, spanning from Spain to Portugal.

* Today, in Spain, the horses are registered as Pure Spanish Horses or P.R.E. (Pura Raza Espanola).

* In Portugal, the horses are registered as Pure Portuguese Horses or P.S.L. (Puro Sangue Lusitano).

* An Iberian horse crossed with a draft horse is often called an Iberian Warmblood.

HORSESHOE PITCHING

The game of horseshoes derives from the game of quoits, but uses horseshoes instead of rings. Players take turns throwing the horseshoes at stakes in the ground. Nowadays, stylized U-shaped horseshoes are used, which are about twice the size of an actual horseshoe. The first world championship game was held in 1910 in Boston, Kansas.

Large stylized horseshoes are used in modern games of horseshoe pitching.

Coats of Many Colors

The domesticated horse has an extremely wide variety of coat colors and markings.

A traditional Russian clay whistle in the form of a colorful horse.

+ Horse base colors are black and chestnut (reddish brown). Most other colors, including bay and brown, are created when one of these base-color pigments has a diluting gene, or modifying gene.

+ There are a few breeds that are called colored breeds because they are registered in a breed organization according to their color, not necessarily their heritage. Examples are the Palomino,

Pinto, and Buckskin. Some horses can be registered in two breed registries—for example, Morgan/Buckskin, Quarter Horse/Buckskin, Morgan/Palomino, half-Arabian/Pinto, Saddlebred/Pinto.

+ Duns (diluted reddish, flesh color) can exhibit dun factors—zebra marks, leg barring, shoulder stripes, a mask, and dark ear tips.

DO ALBINOS EXIST?

★ *Genetically, there are no true albinos because the albinism gene is lethal.*

★ *There are white horses that can have dark or blue eyes.*

★ *White-looking horses may result from the breeding of a Cremello (horse with dilution genes). Most Cremellos have a yellowish tint.*

★ *A sabino Pinto (with a gene for removing pigment) may produce a horse that appears pure white. Some of these white horses are born dead or deaf.*

★ *Gray horses, usually born dark, have a gene similar to humans that whitens hair over time. Just like humans, not all grays go totally white.*

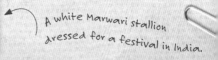

A white Marwari stallion dressed for a festival in India.

Some Common Coat Colors

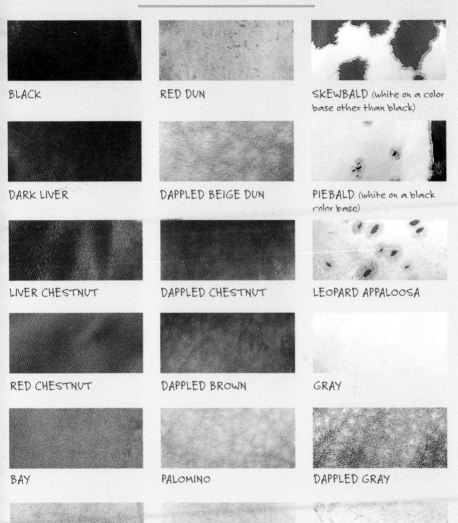

BLACK

RED DUN

SKEWBALD (white on a color base other than black)

DARK LIVER

DAPPLED BEIGE DUN

PIEBALD (white on a black color base)

LIVER CHESTNUT

DAPPLED CHESTNUT

LEOPARD APPALOOSA

RED CHESTNUT

DAPPLED BROWN

GRAY

BAY

PALOMINO

DAPPLED GRAY

ROSE ROAN

CREAM OR CREMELLO

FLEABITTEN GRAY

* If there is any doubt about the color of a horse, it is decided by the color of the points—the muzzle, tips of the ears, mane and tail, and lower part of the legs. For example, a bay has black points (black mane, tail, and legs from the knee down).

Literary Horses

Horses have played starring roles in many works of literature. Here are a few of them:

+ **Artax**—Atreyu's horse in *The Neverending Story* (1979) by Michael Ende.

+ **Binky**—Ridden by Death in the *Discworld* series by Terry Pratchett (first book published 1983).

+ **The Black** (title character), **Satan** (firstborn son), **Bonfire** (second son), **Black Minx** (firstborn daughter), and **Flame** (The Black's most dangerous rival)—*The Black Stallion* series by Walter Farley (first book published 1941).

+ **Black Beauty**—*Black Beauty: The Autobiography of a Horse* (1877) by Anna Sewell.

+ **Boxer** (naive draft horse), **Clover** (Boxer's draft horse friend), and **Mollie** (vain white mare)—*Animal Farm* (1945) by George Orwell.

+ **Breehy-hinny-brinny-hoohy-hah (Bree)** and **Hwin**—Talking horses in *The Horse and His Boy* (1954) by C.S. Lewis, the fifth novel in *The Chronicles of Narnia* series.

+ **Condor**—The mount of the Green Rider Karigan G'ladheon in the *Green Rider* series by Kristen Britain (first novel published 1998).

+ **Flicka** and **Thunderhead**—*My Friend Flicka* (1941) and *Thunderhead, Son of Flicka* (1943) by Mary O'Hara.

+ **The Houyhnhnms**—a race of intelligent horses in *Gulliver's Travels* (1726) by Jonathan Swift.

+ **Lark**—Ridden by an orphan girl escaping from a totalitarian government in *The Berserker's Horse* (1995) by Lisa Maxwell.

+ **Misty of Chincoteague**—*Misty of Chincoteague* (1947), the story of a real pony by Marguerite Henry.

+ **Nara**—Magical horse in *The Dark Horse* series by Mary H. Herbert (first book published 1990).

+ **The Pie**—The horse ridden to victory by a young girl, Velvet Brown, in the Grand National steeplechase in *National Velvet* (1935) by Enid Bagnold.

+ **Rocinante**—The horse ridden by the title character in *Don Quixote* (1605 and 1616) by Cervantes.

+ **Silver Blaze**—Stolen racehorse recovered by the great detective in *The Memoirs of Sherlock Holmes* (1894) by Arthur Conan Doyle.

Engraving by Gustave Doré showing Don Quixote riding Rocinante while attacking windmills, which he mistook for ferocious giants.
The phrase "tilting at windmills" now means an act of futility.

THE RED PONY
John Steinbeck's classic novella *The Red Pony* is episodic, meaning that each chapter can stand alone as a short story.

BLACK BEAUTY AND HORSES' RIGHTS

Black Beauty, the 1877 classic novel, was the only book written by author Anna Sewell. Her motivation for the book was to promote the humane treatment of horses.

This 1865 newspaper illustration helped rally support for the founding of the American Society for the Prevention of Cruelty to Animals the following year.

FOX HUNTS

A huntsman and his foxhounds.

* The sport of fox hunting originated in Britain in the 1500s, and eventually reached most countries worldwide.

* Fox hunting involves the locating, chasing, and killing of a red fox by a group of riders and their trained foxhounds.

* The Master of Foxhounds is in charge of leading with the dogs.

* The riders are divided into groups. The First Field group takes the direct, challenging route that may involve jumping. The Second Field group takes the longer, less rigorous route.

* In 2004, fox hunting was banned in England and Wales through the activist efforts of those who felt the sport was cruel and unnecessary.

* In the United States, the sport is now called fox chasing. The fox is chased (for the thrill of the chase), but not killed.

Hay Forms

Hay comes in several different forms.

Hay lifting—who needs a gym?

Bales

Hay can come in gigantic round bales, weighing about 800–1200 pounds (360–540 kg); large, heavy rectangular bales weighing about 200 pounds (90 kg); and standard rectangular bales weighing about 50–75 pounds (22–34 kg), which is easy for one person to handle.

Flakes

When you break off a section of hay, it is called a flake. Flakes can weigh different amounts, so it is considered wise to weigh the hay to make sure that the horse receives adequate amounts. Invest in an inexpensive hay scale.

polypropylene twine is durable and rot-proof.

Save Twine

Baling twine is great to have around for emergencies, and can be used to create a makeshift halter and lead rope.

Cubes, wafers, and pellets

Different hay types (legumes and grasses), along with a small percentage of grains, can be mixed and processed into bite-sized 2-inch (5-cm) cubes, wafers (similar to crackers), and pellets (about the size of a bullet), or chopped into 1-inch (2.5-cm) stems and mixed with molasses (to reduce dust). Horses have been known to choke on cubes.

Pellets

BREED REGISTRIES

Breed is a generalized term for a set population of horses with like genealogy. Most breeds have registries or stud books.

The "General Stud Book" is the registry for the Thoroughbred breed.

IMPRINTING BABIES

Controversy still exists over the value of imprinting, a training method involving the extensive handling of newborn foals within the first hours of birth.

- Imprinting involves using mild constraint to rub and massage the foal's body, with special attention given to the muzzle, ears, legs, rectum, and reproductive parts.
- Advocates believe this is the critical time to have a horse bond with humans, submit to humans, and become less sensitive to stimuli, eventually becoming easier to break and train.
- Some professionals claim to see no difference between imprinted and non-imprinted foals as they age, other than the fact that some seem too confident with humans, to the point of being pushy and disrespectful.

UNIQUE OLYMPIC SPORT

Since 1912, three disciplines of equestrian sport have been on the Olympic program: jumping, dressage, and eventing. It is unlike most Olympic sports in that men and women compete on equal terms, and it involves a strong mutual relationship between two athletes of different species: horse and rider.

Sound Smart

IT IS CORRECT TO SAY A FOAL IS "OUT OF" THAT MARE AND "BY" THAT STALLION, BUT NEVER THE OTHER WAY AROUND—IT IS PHYSICALLY IMPOSSIBLE FOR A FOAL TO COME OUT OF A MALE.

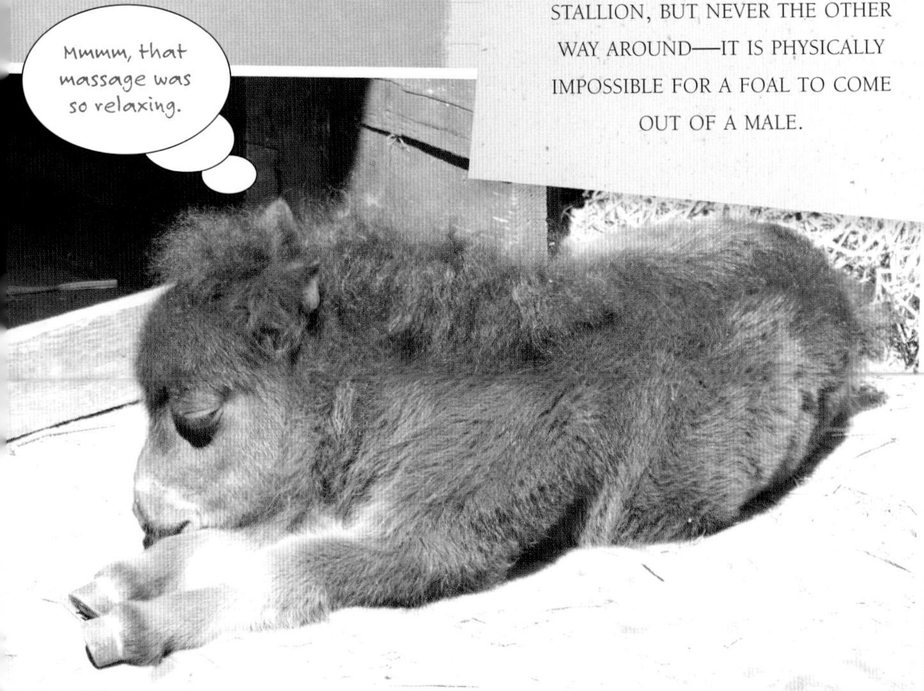
Mmmm, that massage was so relaxing.

Dressage Courts

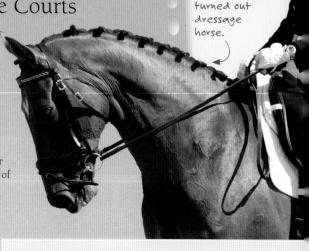

A beautifully turned out dressage horse.

+ A dressage arena is called a court. There are two sizes: small and standard. The small court is 20 x 40 m (20⅞ x 43¾ yards). A standard full-size Olympic dressage court is 20 x 60 m (20⅞ x 65⅝ yards).

+ The court is often used with markers (letters) to remember where to execute movements of a pattern. These markers also help the judge to assess how precisely a movement has been made, demonstrating harmony between horse and rider.

+ No one knows for sure how the letters around the dressage court originated, but a popular theory is that each is the initial letter of a courtier's rank in imperial Germany, with the order of the letters going from the top rank downward.

Learn Your Letters

Remember the letters (A, K, E, H, C, M, B, and F) around the smaller dressage court by learning these acronyms:

CLOCKWISE

- *A*ll *K*ing *E*dward's *H*orses *C*an *M*anage *B*ig *F*ences.
- *A K*indly *E*lephant *H*as *C*rushed *M*y *B*linking *F*oot!

COUNTERCLOCKWISE

- *A F*at *B*lack *M*other *C*at *H*as *E*ight *K*ittens.

Watch Yourself

MANY TRAINING FACILITIES HAVE GIGANTIC MIRRORS NEXT TO THE DRESSAGE COURTS, SO RIDERS CAN SEE FOR THEMSELVES IF THEY ARE RIDING CORRECTLY.

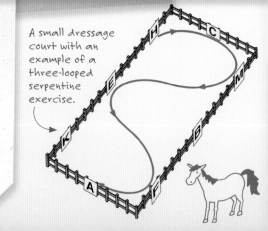

A small dressage court with an example of a three-looped serpentine exercise.

Grulla (blue dun) foal

HORSES ARE MIRRORS

Horses are instinctually reactive, and they are known to mirror human emotions. If a handler is angry, the horse usually becomes angered and defensive. If a handler is calm and relaxed, or quick and tense, the horse tends to react likewise.

Lucky Horseshoes

Horseshoes are considered good luck if they are mounted with the ends upward to hold in the good luck.

This way up

LESSONS AND LEASES VS. OWNERSHIP

★ Horse ownership can be a weighty commitment of finances and time. Serious evaluation of the pros and cons of horse ownership is wise. Impulsive purchases, as often seen with Easter bunny rabbits, Christmas puppies, and other pets, can be a grave mistake. If a child is to get a horse, it is important that he or she has a deep and genuine horse interest (the horse bug); otherwise, the interest may fade, and the parents may be stuck with a horse that needs a good home. It is a lot easier to unload a bunny rabbit.

★ It might be wise to take your child for riding lessons for about six months prior to looking into a horse purchase. This will help to ascertain whether there is a genuine interest in horses that will be longterm, and not just a whim or fantasy.

★ Why not inquire with a reputable horse trainer about leasing or half-leasing (sharing with someone else) a horse? After a substantial time period, parents can see if their child is truly going to stick with the commitments that accompany horse ownership.

Lessons and leasing are good ways of evaluating whether a child has a longterm interest in horses.

Biological Classification

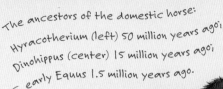

The ancestors of the domestic horse: Hyracotherium (left) 50 million years ago; Dinohippus (center) 15 million years ago; early Equus 1.5 million years ago.

Kingdom:	Animalia
Phylum:	Chordata
Subphylum:	Vertebra
Class:	Mammalia
Subgenus:	

Equus
(the domestic horse
is *Equus caballos*)

Hyppotigris
(zebras)

Asinus
(African asses)

Henionis
(Asian asses)

Brumbies in Kakadu National Park, Australia.

What Is a Feral Horse?

HORSES, SUCH AS THE AMERICAN MUSTANG AND THE AUSTRALIAN BRUMBY, THAT WERE ONCE DOMESTICATED AND THEN ESCAPED TO THE WILD ARE CALLED FERAL HORSES.

GREEK MYTHOLOGICAL HORSES

❖ **Arion** was a speedy immortal horse that was also capable of speech. He was sired by Poseidon, the god of the sea, after Poseidon transformed himself into a stallion.

❖ **Aeos**, **Aetheon**, **Pyrious**, and **Phlegon** were horses that pulled the chariot of Helios, the sun god, across the sky.

❖ **Hippocampus** was a mythical seahorse that pulled the chariot of Poseidon, who was the god of horses as well as of the sea. Hippocampus was often depicted with the front half of a horse and a serpent-like tail.

❖ The **Mares of Diomedes** were four wild man-eating horses. One of the Twelve Labors of Hercules was to steal the mares from the giant Diomedes.

❖ **Sileni** were crude, woodland gods or spirits that were half-man, half-horse.

Hippocampus and mermaid friend.

DRESSAGE: HORSE BALLET

Dressage has its roots in classic Greek horsemanship, and was first recognized in the West during the European Renaissance. True to its Grecian roots, it is a modern-day Olympic event—success is judged through the completion of a set series of movements.

🐴 Horsemeat

✦ The consumption of horsemeat is controversial. Horsemeat is considered a delicacy in many countries, mainly in Europe and Asia, but is a taboo food in others, including the United States, Britain, and Australia.

✦ Activists stand against the inhumane killing (shooting a metal pin into the head, and withdrawing the pin so that the animal bleeds to death in the same way that cattle are slaughtered) versus humane euthanizing by lethal injection, as done with cats and dogs.

✦ Activists emphasize that, throughout the ages, horses have served as battle steeds, transportation, farm workers, companions, and sources of recreation and sport.

✦ Cherry blossom, a Chinese delicacy, is actually raw horsemeat.

The Four Horsemen of the Apocalypse

The Four Horsemen of the Apocalypse are cited in chapter 6 of the book of Revelation in the Christian Bible. Representing the forces of humankind's destruction, they are loosely described according to their powers.

Late 15th-century woodcut by Albrecht Dürer depicting the Four Horsemen of the Apocalypse in "The Revelation of St. John."

A white horse bears a conquering horseman, who carries a bow and wears a crown, which some believe symbolizes victory.

A red horse carries a warrior holding a sword; the color of the horse is often interpreted as blood shed in battle.

A black horse bears a horseman carrying a scale for measurement, which some believe symbolizes famine, desolation, and economic corruption.

A pale green horse carries a rider named Death; some interpret the horse's color as the paleness of death and decay.

Boer Horses

THE BRITISH ARMY USED OVER 500,000 HORSES DURING THE BOER WAR (1899–1902). UNFORTUNATELY, 347,000 OF THE HORSES DIED IN THE WAR. AT LEAST 100 HORSES DIED WHILE BEING SHIPPED DURING OCEAN STORMS.

Helmets: Every Horse, Every Ride

There are diehard advocates of helmet usage who firmly believe that a helmet should be worn by every rider (regardless of ability level), on every horse (regardless of training level), everywhere (even riding down the trails). Here are the reasons why:

+ Sixty percent of all riding accidents leading to death are due to head injuries.

+ The best of horses can trip and unexpectedly fall to the ground with a rider. A fall on a horse that is standing still or walking can be just as dangerous as when the horse is moving.

+ Jumping, breaking young horses, speed events, and so on have an even higher risk of accidents.

+ Most trainers require students under the age of 18 to wear a helmet, even though the dangers can be just as great for adults (many of whom would rather not mess up their hair).

+ Bike helmets and skateboard helmets do not provide adequate protection. All helmets should be made specifically for horses and should have a label that says they are approved by a recognized standards organization—A.S.T.M. (American Society for Testing & Materials) or S.E.I. (Safety Equipment Institute) in the United States; P.A.S. (Product Approved Specification) in Britain; European Normes (E.N.) in Europe; A.S. (Australian Standards) or S.N.Z. (Standards New Zealand) in Australasia.

+ Helmets come in a variety of fun colors and patterns that encourage their use.

+ It is estimated that head-related injuries have decreased by 50 percent in the U.S. since certified helmets have been used.

FITTING A HELMET

* First, check for any cracks or weak points.

* Make sure that the helmet is the right size; it should be a snug, yet comfortable, fit. To test snugness, the forehead skin and eyebrows should move when the helmet is wiggled.

* The helmet should be parallel to the ground, not tipped forward or back. The straps need to be balanced and snuggly secured for the helmet to remain level.

A riding helmet with straps.

Trendy Tails

+ Breeds such as Andalusians, Friesians, and Morgans have full, thick tails and manes.

+ Certain breeds have skimpy tails and manes. Old-time Appaloosas had skimpy tails, known as rat tails. This characteristic has been bred out of the Appaloosas of the present day.

+ The top of a horse's tailbone is called the dock. The tailbone is about 1 foot (30 cm) in length, projecting hair that may reach, or drag, on the ground.

+ Clydesdales, and a few other breeds, may have their tailbones cut short (docked like a dog's tail). A rubber band device cuts off circulation until the lower portion of the tail dies.

+ Saddlebreds often have their tail nerves surgically altered. The tails are put in a special harness to train them to stand upright, making the horse appear proud and explosive.

+ Some horse breed competitions allow wigs (tails from other horses) to be added to a horse's skimpy tail. Full tails can cost up to a few thousand dollars.

+ Hair extensions can be woven into a show horse's tail.

+ It is not uncommon for horses, especially young ones, to chew off the manes and tails of other horses.

The full, flowing tail of this Akhal-teke stallion looks wonderful against the metallic sheen of its coat, and contrasts strikingly with the shaven mane.

Hot Stuff
Put cayenne pepper on a horse's mane or tail to deter hair-chewing.

I can see you if I move my head.

Focus Fix

WHEREAS HUMANS HAVE SELF-ADJUSTING EYE LENSES, HORSES MUST MOVE THEIR HEADS TO ADJUST THEIR LENSES. TO SEE FAR AWAY, A HORSE WILL RAISE ITS HEAD (FOR EXAMPLE, WHEN APPROACHING A JUMP). TO SEE CLOSE IN FRONT, A HORSE WILL LOWER ITS HEAD AND BRING IN ITS NOSE (WHEN WALKING OVER A LOG, FOR INSTANCE).

TAIL BRAIDS

There are many interesting types of tail braids and mud knots (where a braided tail is tied in a knot below the tailbone to protect it from the mud). They are used on horses for functional or aesthetic reasons.

sections from each side of the tail have been braided neatly down the center.

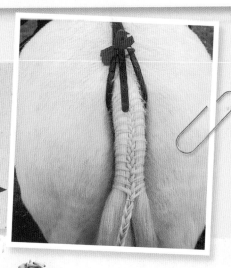

Bones

+ Most horses have about 205 bones in their body.

+ Most horses have 18 ribs, 6 lumbar vertebrae, and 18 tail vertebrae. However, one of the oldest breeds of horses, the Arabian, can have just 17 ribs, 5 lumbar vertebrae, and 16 tail vertebrae.

Horse skeleton

old tin toy of a wind-up horse race.

SIZE OF JOCKEYS

* Most countries typically allow jockey weights of around 135 pounds (61 kg). However, weight limits are sometimes under 120 pounds (54 kg) in the United States, although the Kentucky Derby is set at 126 pounds (57 kg).

* Lighter jockeys are more readily hired, which leads to a high percentage of jockeys with eating disorders (stimulant drugs, plastic suits for exercise, long periods in sauna, purging).

* Although there are no height limits, jockeys tend to be very short because of the weight limits.

IT'S A CINCH

+ Be smart when you tighten the saddle's cinch (western term) or girth (English term). Take your time, and gently, gradually tighten the cinch to the point that it is snug, but not pinching the skin. Imagine someone quickly tightening your belt, and the pain it could cause.

+ Horses that have their cinches tightened too quickly get defensive (cinchy or girthy). Once pinched, they can quickly pick up this habit of squirming and nipping at the person who is trying to tighten the cinch.

+ Cinchy horses will blow up the heart girth area and stomach with air, in anticipation of getting pinched. Then, when they release the air, the saddle is loose. For this reason, it is standard practice to check the cinch again for proper fit, right before you mount the horse.

MINIATURE FARMS

Just as doll enthusiasts enjoy building realistic-looking dollhouses, and stocking them with miniature versions of furniture and decorations, Miniature Horse breeders often enjoy a similar fascination. Horse barns, pastures, jump courses, and equipment are all scaled down to about a quarter normal size. Miniature horse blankets, bridles, and saddles can all be stored in a tiny tackroom. Pasture fences are often so low that the workers can easily step over the fences rather than open gates. One can experience a feeling of being in the land of Lilliputia when visiting one of these miniature farms.

...then carefully tighten and tie off the end.

Buckle the cinch loosely to start...

How to Check a Horse's Vital Signs

❶ PULSE

Normal pulse is 40–50 beats per minute for horses over two years old (higher for foals and excited, nervous horses).

✛ Find the pulse under the front left of the jawbone, where there is a major artery that protrudes slightly.

✛ Press a forefinger on the artery and use a clock or timer to count the beats for 15 seconds. Multiply by 4 to find beats per minute.

✛ Alternatively, take the pulse behind the left elbow with a stethoscope, counting each "lub-dub" as one beat.

❷ HYDRATION

Dehydrated horses may be sick horses. Do a pinch test on the skin of the neck. After pinching, if the skin flattens back into place within a second, the horse is fine. The longer the skin stays pinched before flattening, the more dehydrated the horse is.

❹ RESPIRATION RATE

The normal adult respiration rate is 8–15 breaths per minute. Watch or feel the horse's ribcage/belly for one minute. Count one inhale and one exhale as one complete breath. You can also watch or feel the nostrils.

❸ TEMPERATURE

Normal body temperature is 99–101°F (37.2–38.3°C). Use a digital or mercury thermometer with a long string attached (to avoid losing it).

✛ Shake the thermometer until the mercury level goes lower than 99°F (37.2°C). Lubricate the end of it.

✛ With the horse tied or held, stand to the side of its hindquarter and move the tail aside.

✛ Slowly insert the thermometer into the rectum. Leave in for three minutes (less for digital thermometers).

✛ Read, and then sterilize the thermometer to avoid passing disease.

❺ GUT SOUNDS

Healthy horses have gut sounds; an absence of sounds may indicate colic (stomach problems). Press an ear against the horse's barrel (belly) behind the last rib. Check both sides.

Check the vital signs regularly to learn what is normal for your horse.

In heraldry, the unicorn has a spiral horn, a lion's tail, and a goat's beard and cloven hooves.

UNICORNS: FACT OR FICTION?

★ Unicorns are mythical creatures, usually white, with a single horn on the forehead.

★ They often symbolize purity, chastity, virtue, and virginity.

★ Unicorns are mentioned in the Bible in Numbers 23:22 and 24:8, and in the novel, *Harry Potter and the Sorcerer's Stone*.

★ The unicorn's horn is said to have strong medicinal powers.

★ The famous Carthusian line of Andalusian horses, bred by Carthusian monks, is said to have occurrences of one or two small hornlike growths on the forehead or ear.

Adoption

+ In the United States alone, there are close to 30,000 wild horses and burros (wild donkeys). They are protected by the government's Bureau of Land Management.

+ In New Zealand and many other countries, there are similar governmental organizations that protect wild herds, and also place them for adoption and domestication as riding horses. The Kaimanawa Wild Horses of New Zealand are related to the Exmoor Ponies of England, and are becoming well-known as hardy riding ponies.

+ In some countries, there are prison programs that incorporate wild horses into the rehabilitation of inmates, who are trained to handle and break the horses in an effort to develop patience, purpose, and communication skills.

Wild horses are being used in rehabilitation programs for prisoners.

You can see the white of this Appaloosa's eye.

HUMAN EYES

The sclera, or the white of the eyeball, does not usually show in horses. Throughout the world, it is usually considered an unattractive trait, even though there are occasional individuals within any breed that exhibit the characteristic. The Appaloosa and Pony of the Americas are the rare exceptions in that their registries encourage the breeding of this unique trait.

FIT FOR A QUEEN

In Irish mythology, Embarr (imagination) was the horse of Niamh, one of the queens of Tir na Nog, the land of eternal youth. The horse could run across land and sea without touching them.

Leg Markings

Leg markings are usually described by the highest point of the horse's leg that is covered by white. So, for example, if the white only reaches the coronet, then the horse has coronet leg markings. The color of the hoof usually corresponds to the coronet color. However, a horse with the leopard gene, such as an Appaloosa, may have striped hooves even if leopard markings are not visible on the coronet.

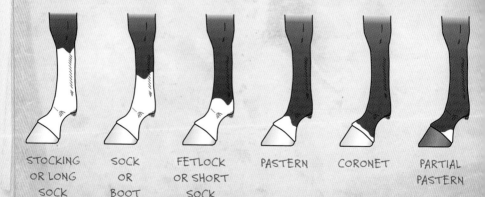

STOCKING OR LONG SOCK

SOCK OR BOOT

FETLOCK OR SHORT SOCK

PASTERN

CORONET

PARTIAL PASTERN

The Lusitano is a heavily muscled but extremely well-balanced Baroque horse.

FOUNDERED

+ Founder is a term used to describe chronic changes in the structure of the foot. These changes are often linked to the painful foot condition laminitis, in which the laminae membranes that hold the bone in place inside the foot become inflamed. In cases of founder, the coffin bone can rotate and/or sink.

+ Just like colic (stomach ache), founder is an ailment that can have life-threatening consequences.

+ Horses may founder when overworked, overheated, or overfed.

+ Blood circulation is quickly altered, causing damage to cells in the legs, and sometimes crippling the horse for life.

Go for Baroque

Strong, heavily muscled, yet agile European horse breeds, traditionally used for classical riding, are commonly called Baroque horses. Lipizzaners, Lusitanos, Andalusians, and Friesians are all Baroque horses.

FURLONG
The racing term furlong is ⅛ mile (201 m).

RIDING DOUBLE

* Some horses resent having two riders on their back, but can usually be trained to accept it.

* The resentment may come from pain. The second rider usually sits near the horse's loins behind the ribcage, supported solely by the backbone.

* Saddles exist that are made with two seats, to allow an adult to ride with a child. Specialized ones are made for therapeutic riding to allow an instructor to guide the horse for the student who has a disability.

Eating little and often will help avoid stomach trouble.

A Stomach Ache Can Get Serious

Colic (stomach ache) is a major cause of horse deaths. The horse's small stomach (about 10 percent of the digestive system) requires that a horse graze and eat small, frequent meals. If a horse overeats, or eats bad feed, high levels of digestive gases can paralyze the muscle that allows food to continue through the digestive tract. This blockage can cause the stomach to rupture. If a horse starts rolling on the ground in pain, the intestines can get twisted, also causing ruptures. If a veterinarian cannot handle the problem with treatments, expensive surgeries are sometimes successful.

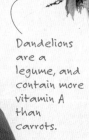

Dandelions are a legume, and contain more vitamin A than carrots.

Diet Lingo

✦ Hay is also known as forage or roughage.

✦ There are two hay classifications: grasses and legumes (high protein, less moisture).

✦ Grains are also known as concentrates or cereal grains.

✦ Special nutritional products are known as supplements.

My, What Big Eyes You Have!

The horse is considered to have the largest eyes of any land animal, except the ostrich.

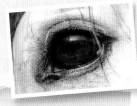

Horse

Ostrich

FUN AT THE BEACH?

Running a horse down the beach, along the coastline, or through the sand sounds very exciting and somewhat romantic. However, such activity is extremely stressful on the horse's tendons and ligaments, with the possibility of leading to serious lameness issues. Always be aware of the footing wherever you ride, especially outside of the arena.

A carriage rider on Dunedin Beach, New Zealand.

Will I Be Tall Like Mom and Dad?

It is difficult to project how tall a horse will be. Poor nutrition can make a horse smaller than its genetic code, but good nutrition cannot make a horse taller. There are, however, some widespread theories that some horsemen use to predict the future adult size of a foal. Two disputable formulas are as follows:

How tall will this newborn filly grow?

Hock

Elbow

Knee

Coronet

Ergot

Cannon

Cannon Bone

✦ This is the long, cannon-shaped bone below the knees and hocks. In a horse with good conformation, the cannon bones should not be too long or light.

✦ It is believed that in order to support a 1,000-pound (450-kg) horse, the cannon bones should be at least 7–8 inches (18–20 cm) in circumference.

The cannon bone is a major support for the horse's body weight.

❶ **Ergot-to-Elbow Method:** Place the end of a length of string at the fetlock joint (near the ergot, the tubular growth on the back of the fetlock joint, hidden within the hair tuft). Take the rest of the string up to the elbow. Keeping the string on the elbow, double the string by raising the starting end (at ergot) up above the horse. The high point supposedly predicts how tall the horse will become.

❷ **Knee-to-Coronet Method:** Use a cloth measuring tape. Place it at the middle of the knee, or the crease in the knee, and take the other end down to the top of the coronet band of the hoof. The measurement in inches is supposedly equivalent to the future height measured in hands—that is, 15 inches equal 15 hands, 15¼ inches equal 15.1 hands, 15½ inches equal 15.2 hands, 15¾ inches equal 15.3 hands, 16 inches equal 16 hands, and so on.

A mare and her
foal grazing in
mountain pastures.

Mane Forelock

Manes and Forelocks

✦ The forelock is the portion of the mane that grows between the ears and over the face.

✦ Forelocks and manes aid in protection from flies and insects, and can be tossed like a fly swatter.

✦ Not all horses can grow a long, luxurious mane and tail. Just like humans, you either have great hair genes or you do not.

✦ Some horses grow manes that pass the shoulders and knees, and tails that drag on the ground.

✦ Braids can be used to keep a long mane safe from breakage, and from getting tangled in the reins and rider's hands.

✦ When loved horses die, some owners cut off the horse's forelock to keep as a memento.

✦ Reins for hackamore bridles, western saddle cinches, and grooming brushes are often made out of woven horsehair.

Ardennes Draft Horse

A Belgian Draft Horse with braided mane, forelock, and tail.

A horse cribbing on a fence post.

COMMON HORSE VACCINES

Horses are routinely vaccinated for the prevention of the following diseases:

✳ **Rabies**—An infectious viral disease that affects the central nervous system.

✳ **Tetanus**—A paralytic disease caused by bacterium from the soil or feces that enters wounds.

✳ **Equine Viral Encephalomyelitis**—Transmitted by mosquitoes, this contagious disease causes brain and spinal cord inflammation. There is a western strain (W.E.E.), an eastern strain (E.E.E.), and a Venezuelan strain (V.E.E.).

✳ **Influenza**—A contagious viral disease affecting the upper respiratory tract.

✳ **Strangles**—A contagious bacterial disease that affects the upper respiratory tract and causes abscesses in lymph nodes (especially in the throat area).

✳ **West Nile Virus**—Mosquitoes transmit this disease to horses, humans, birds, and other mammals, often causing swelling of the brain and paralysis.

✳ **Potomac Horse Fever**—A summer disease caused by a rickettsial organism that can result in a high fever, extreme diarrhea, and severe founder.

✳ **Rhinopneumonitis**—
A viral disease that affects the respiratory and circulatory systems, often leading to abortion in pregnant mares.

WHAT A SUCK UP

✦ A cribber is a horse that has the odd habit of pushing down its upper teeth on an object, such as the edge of a feed tub or board, and sucking in air.

✦ This sucking in of air is thought to have a euphoric effect on the horse, and is believed to be initiated by boredom.

✦ Cribbing collars can be placed on the horse's neck to prevent the horse from widely opening the airway. However, the habit is extremely hard to break.

LIFE EXPECTANCY

✪ Until recent years, the life expectancy of a horse was usually 20–25 years.

✪ With advances in health care, it is now common for a horse to live to an average of 25–30 years of age.

✪ Claims exist that the oldest ever horse was Old Billy, an English draft horse who died in 1822 at the age of 62.

Vaccination certificates should consist of both written and diagrammatic identification of the horse.

THE ARABIAN

The horse we now call the Arabian or Arab has probably influenced more other breeds of horse and pony than any other in the world. Romanticized for its beauty, spirit, intelligence, and affectionate disposition, the Arabian is also respected for its toughness, individuality, and stamina. Claimed to be the oldest and purest breed, the Arabian is a riding horse without equal. Its legendary stamina makes it a superb long-distance riding horse, and it excels in endurance events.

The traditional horse of the desert, the Arabian is known as the "Drinker of the Wind."

National Symbols

Only two countries in the world have a horse as their national animal. Canada has the Canadian Horse (and the beaver), and the United Arab Emirates has the Arabian.

POPULAR BREEDS FROM AUSTRALIA, ASIA, AND AFRICA

- Akhal-Teke
- Arabian or Arab
- Australian Pony
- Australian Stock Horse
- Barb
- Bashkir
- Caspian
- Przewalski's Horse
- Turkmene

Exercising a racehorse in a swimming pool in the United Arab Emirates.

EXERCISE OPTIONS

Horses can be exercised using the following equipment:

* A treadmill designed for horses.

* A hot walker machine that leads horses around a circle, tied to overhead arms, to exercise them or cool them down after a race or workout (in effect, a clothesline for wet horses).

* A circular moving chute that keeps the horse moving in a compartment similar to a gigantic revolving door.

* A custom-made swimming pool that is adapted for horse use (imagine the pool filters!).

* A lunge line to lunge the horse in large circles, with the handler in the middle (stare at the head, or get dizzy).

ENDURANCE RIDING

+ Sometimes called the sport of a million steps, endurance riding is an international phenomenon, with over 250 international competitions held each year.

+ In Dubai, the United Arab Emirates sponsor the World's Most Preferred Endurance Ride, a 125-mile (200-km) two-day endurance race in the desert.

+ The Tevis Cup is a 100-mile (160-km) trail race from Nevada to California, in less than 24 hours, with one horse. The winning time is typically around 16 hours.

+ The Tom Quilty Gold Cup, patterned after the Tevis Cup, has been called Australia's most punishing endurance race. Riders come from all around the world to participate in the 100-mile (160-km) one-day ride that covers the rugged terrain of Tasmania. A recent winner completed the ride in a little over 11 hours.

+ Endurance riding has been a part of the Asian Games since the 1994 games in Hiroshima, Japan.

Horses are curious animals, a trait that can be utilized in training.

🐎 Horse Sense: IQ

+ Horses have small brains relative to their body size.

+ They should not be compared to animals that are predators, such as dogs and cats. Horses are prey animals and behave differently, according to their flight or fight instincts.

+ Horses are trainable, even though many of a rider's commands contradict their natural instincts.

+ Horses learn through a process of positive and negative reinforcement, involving lots of repetition in small increments of time and content.

+ They remember things very well, often putting an elephant to shame. This can be a problem because they seldom forget and forgive poor training experiences.

+ They recognize sounds pertaining to certain people, feed buckets, vehicles, and so on. They learn to respond to simple verbal cues, such as "whoa," "move on," and "click-click."

+ A belief is that the lower the IQ of a horse, the more submissive the horse is, and the easier it is to train.

+ Some trainers make IQ assessments based on the horse's problem-solving abilities, rate of learning, and retention of knowledge.

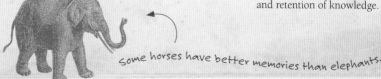

Some horses have better memories than elephants.

Does your horse have strange tastes?

HORSES AND ELECTRICITY

+ Keep all extension cords and outlets away from horses. They love to chew on cords, or play with them.

+ Electric fencing can be a good choice for pastures and large turn-out areas. Many products are available in the form of highly visible fencing strands containing electric elements. Such fencing cannot be chewed or rubbed on, and the horses cannot get their feet or shoes stuck on the fence, as is possible with wire-mesh fencing.

+ Controversial electric shock collars, which are similar to those used on dogs, are now on the market for disciplining horses for certain poor behaviors, such as kicking the stall walls. If considering such an extreme device, consult a professional trainer who knows how to implement the procedure properly.

DID MY HORSE EAT A ROCK?

* Stones may be found in a horse's manure, and it is likely they were created inside the horse's digestive system.

* Intestinal stones (enteroliths) are primarily made up of magnesium, calcium, ammonium, and phosphate.

* The stones are created when the horse ingests a foreign object like sand, wire, or baling twine, and minerals build up around it in rings, layer upon layer.

* Smaller stones can be passed in the feces, but larger stones cannot pass and often end up disrupting digestion, resulting in colic (stomach ache). A large stone can be lethal when it leads to the rupturing of the intestinal tract.

* Surgery is the common solution for large stones, which are usually spherical or tetrahedral (having four faces, like a pyramid building block), as large as 3½ feet (1 m) in length and weighing up to 15½ pounds (7 kg).

* Kidney stones are rare in horses. Urinary tract stones are typically found in the bladder, and more commonly in males because of the length of the urethra. Sizes range from 3 to 4 inches (8 to 12 cm).

Take care with horses around electricity.

A DARK HORSE

Lipizzaners (considered one of Europe's oldest breeds) are born black, and gradually turn white. A Lipizzaner that stays dark is considered by some to be good luck.

Tobacco leaves

TOBACCO WARNING

Tobacco leaves are known to be toxic to horses, as well as some potato and tomato plants. Other toxic plants include:

- Avocado
- Azalea
- Black walnut
- Castor beans
- Coffee weed
- Heavenly bamboo
- Larkspur
- Lily of the valley
- Marijuana
- Mustard
- Oak
- Oleander
- Onion
- Poison hemlock
- Privet
- Red maple
- Rhubarb
- Spurge
- Sweet clover
- Water hemlock
- Wild radish

Onion

ARENA ETIQUETTE

When multiple riders ride in an arena, what prevents them from crashing into each other? Well, there are road rules. What if horses are traveling in opposite directions, like cars on a highway?

✱ A widely accepted practice is for horses to pass left shoulder to left shoulder if they are traveling at the same gait (for example, both are trotting).

✱ If horses are traveling at different gaits (one is running and one is walking, for instance), it is common practice to have the faster horse pass on the inside of the arena and let the slower horse stay by the wall. This works because the faster horse can veer to the inside more readily.

✱ Another wise practice is not to stop or back up when riding on the rail (near the wall). This prevents one horse from getting rear-ended by another—and averts a five-horse pile-up.

HORSE MANICURE?

Horse hooves have a similar protein structure to human hair and fingernails. That is why some people actually use horse products on their hair and nails.

Lily of the valley

19th-century etching of the Trojan Horse.

🐎 The Trojan Horse

Historical writings depict the Trojan Horse as a huge, hollow statue that was left in front of the gates of the city of Troy. Mistaking it for a peace offering from the Greeks who were besieging the city, the Trojans moved the horse inside their city walls. During the night, armed Greek soldiers came out of the statue and opened the gates for Greek troops to enter. After fierce fighting, the Greeks were victorious and the Trojan War was at an end. Thus the saying, "Beware of Greeks bearing gifts." The story is told in the Latin epic poem *The Aenid*, written by Virgil in the 1st century B.C.

The Trojan Horse from the 2004 movie "Troy," installed on the seafront at Çanakkale, Turkey, after filming was complete.

Tunisian stamp depicting a 1,700-year-old mosaic showing Virgil, who wrote a poem with the story of the Trojan Horse.

الجمهورية التونسية
REPUBLIQUE TUNISIENNE

600
Mosaïque de Virgile
2002

NORDIC MYTHOLOGICAL HORSES

* **Hofvarpnir** (Hoof Flourisher) was the horse of the goddess Gna. It was capable of moving over water and through the air.

* **Skinfaxi** was the horse of Dagr, god of the daytime, and **Hrimfaxi** was the horse of Nott, goddess of the nighttime. Each horse had a shining mane that lit up the sky for day and night.

* **Sleipnir** (meaning smooth or gliding) was an eight-legged horse belonging to Odin, the chief god of Norse mythology. The swiftest horse on earth, Sleipnir could carry Odin over water, through the air, and to and from Valhalla, the land of the dead.

19th-century paintings by Peter Nicolai Arbo, depicting Dagr riding Skinfaxi (above) and Nott riding Hrimfaxi (left).

18th-century Icelandic illustration of Odin riding the eight-legged Sleipnir.

HORSES OF CAMELOT

Hengroen *and* **Llamrei** *were the horses of King Arthur, the legendary ruler of post-Roman Britain around the 5th to 6th centuries.*

The Ties That Bind

There are various ways to tie a horse, but not all horses cooperate with each method.

+ A direct tie is when the lead rope that is attached to the halter is tied to a hitching rail or ring on a wall. A quick-release slipknot is standard.

+ In cowboy movies, you see riders quickly hop off their horses and WRAP the reins around the hitching post. This is because, if you tie the reins to a hitching post and the horse pulls back, the bit could damage the horse's mouth and tongue.

+ Cross ties are two ropes attached high on opposing walls of a stall or barn aisle. The snaps at the end of the ropes attach to each side of the horse's halter, keeping the horse's head still as the horse stands in the middle.

+ A ground tie is a method whereby the horse is taught to stand untied, with the lead rope or reins dropped to the ground. It takes structured training to get horses to buy into this idea.

Standing Snoozers

✤ BY NATURE, HORSES ARE PREY ANIMALS. ALTHOUGH HORSES MAY LIE DOWN TO SLEEP, DOING SO MAKES THEM VULNERABLE TO PREDATORS.

✤ A LOCKING MECHANISM, CALLED THE STAY APPARATUS, ALLOWS MUSCLES TO REST WHILE TENDONS AND LIGAMENTS LOCK FOR A STANDING STATE OF SLEEP. ONE HINDLEG CAN REMAIN UNLOCKED, BUT NOT A FORELEG.

A horse tied with cross ties in a stall.

Horses tied to a hitching rail with quick-release slipknots.
Note how the horses unlock one hindleg and snooze while standing up.

Twins: Double Trouble

+ Surviving twins are extremely rare—approximately 1 percent of all births.

+ Ultrasound technology reveals that twins are more common in the first 30 days of embryonic growth, with most dying off by the 45th day. After that, 70 percent of twins are usually naturally aborted.

+ Full-term twins often result in one or both dying, or having complications. Some survive to lead productive lives.

+ In 1917 there was a claim that a mare, in nine pregnancies, produced three set of twins. Supposedly, two of the sets were mules, fathered by a donkey.

FEEDING RULE OF THUMB

Feed 1 pound (450 g) of hay to each 100 pounds (45 kg) of horse's body weight per feeding.

QUADRUPLETS!

✦ Advancements in reproduction techniques enable the flushing of a fertilized egg (or eggs) from a mare so that it can be packaged, transported, and transferred into the uterus of a recipient (surrogate) mare.

✦ These embryo transfers allow for successful show horses and racing horses to continue uninterrupted with their careers, yet have multiple babies born.

✦ Normally, a mare can only have one foal per year, so imagine the number of foals that will be possible with embryo transfers.

Twin foals are extremely rare.

We may be twice the trouble, but we're twice as adorable, too.

Blood

Horses typically have around 13.2 gallons (50 l) of blood in their bodies.

Intestinal Fortitude

Full-grown horses have an average of 89 feet (27 m) of intestines.

Missing Pieces

Horses do not have gall bladders or collarbones.

Anatomy of a horse from a 15th-century Egyptian manuscript.

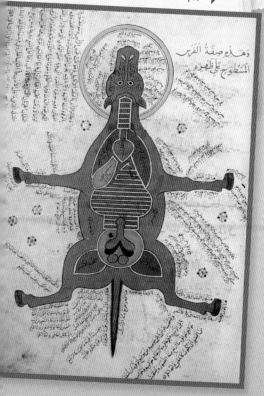

HE'S GONE MARBLES

Many horsemen refer to the negative experiences that are logged into the horse's mind as black marbles. With every bad experience, such as a harsh reprimand or an accident, the horse retains a black marble. When a similar situation arises, that black marble is immediately recalled by the horse. Those marbles remain forever, as well as the fears and emotions that go along with them. This is why wise horsemen should not use forceful, stressful training methods.

WHAT DO HORSES AND RABBITS HAVE IN COMMON?

* Rabbits and horses have very similar digestive systems. Both have a simple stomach, with an extensive intestinal system and an enlarged cecum (the pouch at the beginning of the large intestine), as do guinea pigs and chinchillas.

* You might think that cattle and horses would be more similar, but on the contrary, they have extremely different digestive systems. Cattle are ruminants, with a rumen (the first compartment of the stomach) that provides the capability of regurgitation, or chewing the cud.

A show jumper riding hunt seat.

Riding Styles

The following are the basic styles or seats, each of which has many variations:

+ **Dressage seat**—Used for classical training.

+ **Hunt seat** (considered a form of English riding)—Primarily used for jumping.

+ **Saddle seat** (considered a form of English riding)—Used on animated, high-stepping horses that trot more uphill, such as South African Saddlebreds, American Saddlebreds, Arabians, Morgans, and Hackneys.

+ **Stock seat** (western)—Used for western pleasure, cutting, roping, trail riding, and so on.

Gymkhana

+ The word gymkhana is derived from the Hindi language, and refers to a place where sporting events are held. In India, it is commonly interpreted as a gymnasium. The term is not only used for horse events, but may also include competitions for car racing and gymnastics.

+ Horse gymkhanas usually involve timed pattern races and games. These thrilling speed events may include barrel racing, pole bending, ring spearing, keyhole racing, quadrangle stake racing, two-man relay, and single-pole racing.

+ Rodeos are primarily made up of events for male competitors, so it is not uncommon to have women's barrel racing in conjunction with a rodeo.

A western stock-seat rider and golden Palomino in a single-pole race.

A top hat is worn at upper-level dressage competitions.

Saddle-seat attire

APPROPRIATE TACK AND ATTIRE

The various types of horses require specific tack and attire unique to each purpose.

* **Dressage seat**—It is customary to ride in a dressage saddle, wearing a black hunt cap, black derby or top hat (depending on the level), a black hunt coat or a black dressage coat with tails (shadbelly), a white shirt (ratcatcher shirt), a stock tie with pin (ascot), white breeches, long, black dressage boots, and black gloves.

* **Hunt seat**—Competitors ride in a hunt saddle, wearing a hunt cap, a white shirt (ratcatcher shirt) with stock tie and pin, a hunt coat, breeches, and black dress or field boots.

* **Saddle seat**—It is customary to ride in a flat saddle (cutback saddle), wearing a rolled derby, conservative saddle suit or more colorful daycoat with complementary pants (jodhpurs), collared shirt with a long tie, and short jodhpur boots.

* **Stock seat**—In most competitions, riders use a western saddle and wear a western hat, long-sleeved shirt, small scarf or pin, jeans, belt, chaps, and western boots. There tends to be a lot of variation and change in show tack and attire (especially among female riders), with expensive silver and tooling added to the saddles and bridles. The other types of riding tend to be more constant and traditional.

RIDING DISCIPLINES

Besides riding a particular style or seat (stock seat, hunt seat, dressage seat, or saddle seat), there are many riding specialties or disciplines, including:

- Competitive trail riding
- Cutting
- Driving
- Endurance trail riding
- Eventing
- Fox hunting
- Jumping
- Polo
- Racing
- Reining
- Rodeo
- Roping
- Show pleasure
- Show trail
- Vaulting

Black dress boots

Western boots

Those Adorable Dimples

SOME HORSES HAVE WHAT ARE KNOWN AS MUSCLE DIMPLES OR PROPHET'S THUMBS, WHICH ARE INDENTATIONS IN THE MUSCLES, USUALLY ON THE NECK. A BELIEF IS THAT THEY ARE THE RESULT OF MUSCLE DAMAGE OR INJURY.

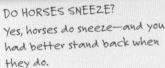

DO HORSES SNEEZE?
Yes, horses do sneeze—and you had better stand back when they do.

FEAR OF WATER

* Most horses will choose to go around a puddle or body of water, rather than walk through it.

* If a horse will not go through water, have another horse lead the way. The herd instinct might encourage the balking horse to follow.

A boy leads a nervous horse across a river.

Oh, Horsefeathers!

- Horsefeathers is a slang term meaning absurd and nonsensical, thought to be first used in a political cartoon, "Barney Google," written by William De Beck.

- It is the name of a 1932 Marx Brothers film.

- The Friesian breed of horse is sometimes called the feathered horse, because of the long hairs on the lower leg that resemble feathers.

- Many draft breeds have these long hairs, called feathering.

The Friesian has a profuse wavy mane and tail, and feathering on the legs. It is prized as a carriage horse, with remarkable trotting ability.

Feathering

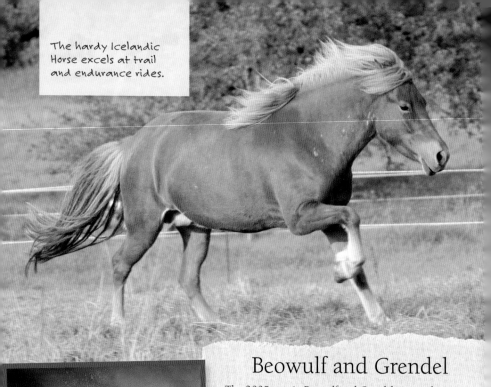

The hardy Icelandic Horse excels at trail and endurance rides.

Beowulf and Grendel

The 2005 movie *Beowulf and Grendel* received negative comments from critics about the actors riding horses that were too small for them. Actually, authenticity was the purpose for this. Purebred Icelandic Horses, descendants of ponies from 9th-century Europe, were used in the film, just as they were originally used by Viking warriors. These noble war horses were said to rescue their fallen riders by laying down for the injured warrior to crawl on, safely taking them home using their incredible homing sense.

Many people believe that horses can sense weather phenomena such as volcanic eruptions.

STORM PREDICTORS?

It is commonly reported that horses exhibit odd behavior (flighty and distracted) prior to storms, volcanic eruptions, earthquakes, and tsunamis. Some believe this phenomenon may be related to ultrasonic waves or electromagnetic signals. Before one major volcanic eruption at Mount St. Helens in the U.S., a herd of horses was reported to have safely migrated away from the area, prior to the eruption.

Street Smarts

A horse's legs can become damaged by hard street surfaces.

+ Riding on hard, slick streets can be dangerous, especially if horses do not wear proper traction shoes (borium). They can slip on the hard surface with a rider.

+ The concussion on the hard surface can damage a horse's bones and tendons, so it is best only to walk a horse, not trot or run, on such a hard surface.

+ Special concussion pads can be nailed between the foot and shoe to help absorb the shock to the horse's legs.

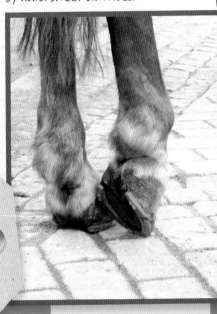

FEEDING ON THE GROUND
Many horsemen feed their horses at ground level in the belief that this natural grazing position is good for the horse's back and neck muscles.

A horse's natural grazing position is at ground level.

FEEDING TIMES

Horses are grazing animals and have small stomachs that require frequent small meals to avoid digestive problems. Unfortunately, domesticated horses that are kept in confined areas are often fed according to people's schedules, just two or three times a day.

World Games

Every four years, sanctioned by the Fédération Equestre Internationale (F.E.I.), the World Equestrian Games are held as the world championships in eight equestrian sports: show jumping, dressage, eventing, driving, reining, vaulting, endurance, and para-equestrian. In 1990, the inaugural games were held in Stockholm, Sweden. The games have always taken place in Europe, but in 2010 they will be held in Kentucky in the United States.

A horse's natural habit is to graze small amounts of food frequently.

Dala Horse

✦ A Dala, or Dalecarlian, horse is a wooden statue of a horse originating in the Swedish province of Dalarna. There are references to wooden horses for sale dating back to 1623.

✦ Originally made as children's toys, Dala horses have become a national symbol of Sweden.

✦ Dala horses are traditionally painted bright red and decorated with tack painted in white, green, yellow, and blue. A special technique is used involving painting with two colors on the brush at the same time.

✦ One legend claims that the Dala horse is a model of Sleipnir, the eight-legged horse of Odin, the chief god of Norse mythology. However, the Dala horse does not have eight legs.

The Dala horse is the most well-known symbol of Sweden apart from the country's flag.

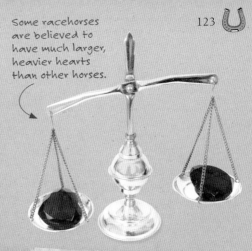

HEART SIZE

* An average horse heart weighs 7–10 pounds (3–4.5 kg).

* The racehorse Phar Lap (1926–1932), known as Australia's wonder horse, is said to have had a heart weighing 14 pounds (6.3 kg). The heart is on display at the National Museum of Australia in Canberra.

* The great American racehorse Secretariat (1970–1989), who still holds several record race times and had a postal stamp in his honor, is rumored to have had a heart weighing 24 pounds (10.8 kg).

* The same thing can be found in human sportspeople. Lance Armstrong, seven-time winner of the Tour de France, the world's biggest cycling race, reportedly has a heart 30 percent larger than most humans.

Some racehorses are believed to have much larger, heavier hearts than other horses.

Roman Riding

Roman riding is a term used for when one rider rides two horses at the same time, standing with one foot on each horse's back. The rider looks like an ancient Roman charioteer, hence the name. Roman riding is a popular entertainment in rodeos and exhibitions.

A Roman riding act from an animal circus around 1914.

Horsey Quotes

* "Horse sense is the best thing a horse has, which keeps it from betting on people." **W.C. Fields**

* "There is something about the outside of a horse that is good for the inside of a man." **Winston Churchill**

* "When you're young and fall off a horse, you may break something. When you're my age, you splatter." **Roy Rogers**

* "A horse! a horse! my kingdom for a horse!" **William Shakespeare,** *Richard III*

* "Treat a woman like a racehorse, and she'll never be a nag." **Anonymous**

* "No hour of life is wasted that is spent in the saddle." **Winston Churchill**

* "Horse, thou art truly a creature without equal, for thou fliest without wings and conquerest without sword." **The Koran**

"O for a horse with wings!"
William Shakespeare, *Cymbeline*

* "Speak your mind, but ride a fast horse." **Anonymous**

* "In buying a horse or taking a wife, shut your eyes tight and commend yourself to God." **Tuscan proverb**

* "Sell the cow, buy the sheep, but never be without the horse." **Irish proverb**

* "A man on a horse is spiritually as well as physically bigger than a man on foot." **John Steinbeck**

* "Don't squat with your spurs on!" **Anonymous**

* "Feeling down? Saddle up." **Anonymous**

* "All I pay my psychologist is the cost of feed and hay, and he'll listen to me all day long." **Anonymous**

* "It's a lot like nuts and bolts. If the rider's nuts, the horse bolts." **Anonymous**

* "Riding—the art of keeping the horse between you and the ground." **Anonymous**

The Horse

Where in this wide world can man
find nobility without pride,

Friendship without envy,

Or beauty without vanity?

Here, where grace is served
with muscle

And strength by gentleness confined

He serves without servility;
he has fought without enmity.

There is nothing so powerful,
nothing less violent.

There is nothing so quick, nothing
more patient.

Ronald Duncan

Paints vs. Pintos

Question: All Paints are Pintos, but not all Pintos are Paints. How can that be?

Answer: Pinto is an American term for horses with large patches of white and another color on their bodies. In other English-speaking countries, this pattern may be referred to as colored. Saddlebreds, Half-Arabians, Miniature Horses, and non-purebred horses can be Pintos. Paints are horses that are predominately of Quarter Horse lineage that are considered to be pinto in color. The American Paint Horse is a breed based on color and lineage. Pintos can be registered as a color breed, regardless of lineage.

This horse has Pinto coloration, but is of Arabian lineage and therefore is not a Paint.

This horse with pinto coloration is of Quarter Horse lineage and is therefore a Paint.

DO YOU SHARE YOUR DRINKING CUP?

+ Consider the disease transmission dangers of allowing your horse to drink out of a community water bucket or water trough.

+ **Disease Prevention Tip:** When filling a series of water buckets for horses in different stalls, do not dip the hose into the water. You will carry microorganisms from one bucket to another.

UNSOUNDNESS

★ Horses are considered unsound when they are lame.

★ Lameness may be temporary when involving stone bruises, abscesses, and minor muscle, ligament, and tendon strains.

★ Serious lameness issues may involve injuries to bones, tendons, and ligaments; bone degeneration (navicular disease, sesamoiditis, arthritis); and founder.

🐎 Bucking Broncos

Not all horses become bucking broncos when getting broke to ride. Much depends on the history of the particular horse, the trainer's skills, and the training methods.

+ Classic dressage principles can be used to avoid making young horses frightened, tense, or rebellious. This usually involves first teaching the horse to long line or ground drive (properly carry a bit in the mouth and steer from the ground).

+ Some primitive breaking methods rely on the rider's brute strength or ability to stay on, whereas most trainers rely on reasoning and the earning of trust.

+ Horses are flight or fight animals. If they cannot get away and are cornered and pressured, they may fight (kick, strike, bite) during the breaking process.

+ Trainers have been known to break horses in the deep snow or a body of water, such as a lake or ocean, where the horse has trouble bucking and rearing.

+ A wide-held belief is that the regular handling of foals and yearlings makes them more trusting, experienced, and submissive; therefore, easier to break.

The rider is no match for this bucking bronco at a rodeo in Australia.

ARENA FOOTING

In the mood for a little horse humor? Check out my glossary.

✳ The extensive and expensive process involved in making an arena that has quality horse footing is now quite scientific. Various layers and sublayers of footing materials must be properly applied at the right depth and slope.

✳ The top layer may consist of various materials, such as finely shredded tires, tennis shoes, or carpet. Many new and innovative footing materials are available that can be mixed with sand or soil to provide a dust-resistant footing that maintains moisture and provides a cushioned, stress-free surface for the horse's legs.

✳ If the footing is too deep, horses may strain their tendons and ligaments. If the footing is too hard, concussion can cause serious bone-related lameness.

Shredded tires and tennis shoes may be used on the floors of arenas.

Music for Horses

◆ Many musical products are available for horses, created on the premise that music can be relaxing.

◆ Soft, melodic soundtracks, minus low and high frequencies (which irritate horses), tend to have a tranquil effect.

◆ Some people play music for their horses during equine massage sessions, farrier visits, vet visits, transporting, and storms.

HORSE GLOSSARY

A BIT: What is left over after a horseman visits a favorite tack shop.

FENCE: A decorative structure built for horses to chew on.

HORSE FEED: A costly substance used to manufacture manure.

RACE: What your heart does when you see your horse's vet bill.

WITHERS: The reason you will seldom see a man riding bareback.

A display of affection and trust between horse and rider.

Best Friends Forever (B.F.F.)

* Horses are very gregarious, and most prefer a companion or buddy.

* Owners can find an older or lame horse, often for free, to make a great companion for a needy horse.

* Some horses form close bonds with ponies, Miniature Horses, donkeys, goats, sheep, dogs, cats, and even chickens.

* If a horse rests its head on your shoulder, this likely indicates trust or affection.

A horse may become close friends with another pet, even a small animal like a cat.

JODHPURS

Jodhpurs, a type of riding breeches that are tight from the knee down, are named after a city in India, where men wore trousers that are similar to today's English riding pants.

Jodhpur in India is known as the "Blue City."

The rider opposite is wearing jodhpurs.

Frank E. Webner, a Pony Express rider, circa 1861, with a Native American woman.

The Pony Express

+ The famous Pony Express mail service across the North American continent spanned 2,000 miles (3,220 km) from Missouri to California.

+ After galloping 10 miles (16 km), day or night, horses were replaced with fresh ones at Pony Express stations.

+ Riders usually rode stints of 75–100 miles (120–160 km).

+ The service lasted only 18 months, from April 1860 to October 1861, when it was replaced by the Intercontinental Telegraph. It was considered one of the United States' greatest business failures.

REMEMBER THE CALCIUM/ PHOSPHORUS RATIO

* To balance the hays and grains in a horse's diet, the calcium to phosphorus ratio ideally needs to be maintained at 2:1.

* Calcium and phosphorus account for approximately 70 percent of the mineral content of the horse's body, with over 80 percent of that amount in the bones and teeth.

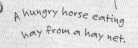

A hungry horse eating hay from a hay net.

TICK OFF

+ Although many horsemen still practice the primitive method of using a lighted cigarette to draw out ticks from a horse, it is not considered wise because it can cause the tick to dispel its stomach contents, resulting in disease transmission.

+ Most disease transmission from a tick occurs within the first 24–36 hours of attachment, so prompt removal is recommended.

+ The most common removal practice is to use tweezers on the tick at the front of its body, as close as possible to the horse's skin surface, and slowly pull out the tick. Be aware that if you grab the rear portion of the tick, it can cause the tick's gut to rupture its infectious contents, and the head may stay within the horse and form a hard nodule (tick bite granuloma). Dispose of the tick and put antiseptic on the wound.

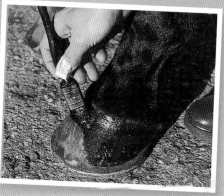

oiling a horse's feet helps to keep the hooves moist and in good condition.

GETTING THE NAILS DONE

Ladies go to a beautician to get their nails done. Well, horses sometimes get their hooves done. Only certain horse competitions allow the hooves to be polished, as part of their rules and regulations. Here is how to get that high-gloss shine on your horse's hooves:

★ Have someone hold the horse on a large rug or rubber mat.

★ Use sandpaper to smooth off the rough, crusty surface of the foot.

★ Use steel wool to buff the surface.

★ Apply a clear wax shoe polish with a rag, and buff dry.

★ Apply black or clear liquid hoof polish (or shoe polish), starting at the coronary band (top of the hoof) and letting it slide down the hoof, quickly smoothing out the liquid.

★ Allow the first coat to dry thoroughly, buff with steel wool, then apply a second coat.

★ Use a hoof polish remover immediately after the competition or parade.

★ It is wise to consider using feed supplements formulated for hoof care, and the regular application of hoof conditioners.

Horse manicure kit: sandpaper, steel wool, and shoe polish.

A Lipizzaner stallion performing a capriole from the hand at the Spanish Riding School in Vienna, 1964.

Flying Horses

In times of warfare, horses were taught to do some extreme athletic maneuvers that involved coming off the ground. The following maneuvers, called airs above the ground, are still taught in classic riding schools throughout the world.

A white stallion performing a levade.

Levade: The horse raises its forelegs off the ground, by crouching onto its haunches and keeping its body at 45 degrees to the ground.

Courbette: The horse does a movement similar to the levade, and then jumps or bounces in that position.

A series of early 20th-century paintings by the Viennese equestrian artist Ludwig Koch.

Croupade: The horse leaps through the air, remaining parallel to the ground and tucking its hindlegs under.

Ballotade: The horse leaps as for a croupade, but holds its hindlegs so that the shoes are visible from behind.

Capriole: The horse appears to fly by leaping through the air, tucking in its forelegs and kicking out with the hindlegs.

Large trailers can accommodate several horses, with plenty of amenities for their comfort.

Any idea where the chauffeur's gone? Shall we call room service?

🐴 Horse Trailers

+ A horse trailer was originally known as a horse box. Today, horse trailers come in all sizes and shapes.

+ Some horse trailers have luxurious, hotel-like living quarters for the owners to stay in during horse competitions and rodeos.

+ Some horses actually ride in the back of pick-up trucks, in the bed with side walls and a loading ramp.

+ It is not uncommon for a pick-up truck to pull a six-horse trailer.

+ Large semi-trucks are used by professional haulers, with the inside of the boxed portion made into as many as 12 padded stalls, with air conditioning, heating, automatic watering systems, and other amenities.

+ Horses that are raised on islands are often exported to the coastlines on ferryboats.

+ When hauling horses, it is standard practice to travel with barrels of the home water to which the horse is accustomed. If they fail to drink during travel, and get dehydrated, they can easily develop colic (stomach ache).

+ Just like athletes, electrolytes are often added to the water of a traveling horse to avoid dehydration.

LOADING AND UNLOADING A HORSE TRAILER

Horses must be taught how to walk up the ramp, or step up into the trailer, and also how to walk or step back down. It takes much patience and many positive training sessions. Quick methods often result in the horse panicking and hurting itself inside the trailer. Horses have incredible memories, and once they have a bad experience in loading or hauling, they are apt to have related issues for the rest of their lives.

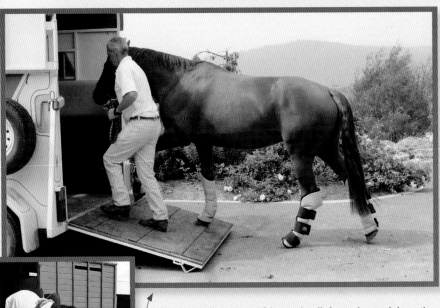

Loading: Always be confident and walk forward toward the trailer in a positive attitude. Keep the horse straight and allow it time to adjust to walking up the ramp. If necessary, try a few sessions with another horse as a companion or encourage it with food, once inside. A little patience and lots of practice are the keys to success.

Unloading: Encourage the horse to move out of the trailer slowly, and let it have a look around before getting out. Do not hurry the horse down the ramp. It may need a few minutes to adjust to the light and its new surroundings once the ramp has been lowered.

Helpful Hint: Air Those Floorboards!

Horses can urinate while traveling, causing water to accumulate between the mats and floorboards. Occasionally, inspect and air out the floorboards of the horse trailer. Horses have been known to fall partially through the floor while in transport.

Horse Cemeteries

★ *Many regions have restrictions or bans on burying horses. If allowed, horses usually must be buried at least 100 feet (30 m) away from a water source, and buried at a depth of 8 feet (2.4 m) in an 8 x 10-foot (2.4 x 3-m) area.*

★ *Dead horses are usually hauled away by paid knackers to rendering plants (knackeries).*

BLIND TRUST

Some horses have been known to continue as riding horses after going blind, trusting in the rider's aids (seat, hands, legs, and voice) to guide them.

Personality Plus

People with limited horse knowledge assume that horses are all the same. Just like humans, however, no two horses are alike.

✦ Some horses are extremely friendly and people-oriented, whereas others are known to be aggressive or standoffish.

✦ Mares (females) tend to be moody and hormonal, or marish.

✦ Stallions (males) tend to be aggressive and sexually driven.

✦ Geldings (castrated males) are often considered to be even-tempered and reliable, and are most widely used for inexperienced riders and in competitions where the horse must focus.

✦ Different horse breeds, just like dog breeds, have temperament qualities that are unique. Draft horses tend to be docile and unflappable, whereas some hotblooded breeds, such as the Arabian and Thoroughbred, can be more reactive.

Some horses seem to display gestures of friendship or sympathy to their companions.

I'm sorry. Please can we be friends again?

Okay, as long as you promise to stop horsing around...

boys who like to wrestle and get rough.

Different breeds of horse are broken to ride at different ages.

Ready to Ride

+ The process of getting a horse to accept being ridden or harnessed is called horse breaking. The best age at which to break a horse varies among breeds and beliefs. It is not uncommon for trainers to break some stock types, saddle-horse types, and racing types—for example, Appaloosas, Quarter Horses, Saddlebreds, and Thoroughbreds—as late yearlings.

+ Many other breeds, including Arabians, Morgans, and Andalusians, are often not ridden until they are three years old, when they are considered more mentally and physically developed.

+ Some larger horses, such as warmbloods, light draft horses, or draft breeds, are often not broken to ride until they are four years old.

+ Many owners get X-rays of the epiphyseal growth plate in the knee of a young horse to determine when the horse is physically ready to be ridden.

+ How a horse reacts to carrying a saddle for the first time may be an indicator of how it may react when it carries a rider for the first time.

Sidesaddle

In previous centuries, female sidesaddle riders would wear dresses to remain "proper" while riding. Horses were even jumped in sidesaddles. Today, there are competitions for this style of riding, using custom-made western or English saddles. Since the rider can only cue from one side with her legs, the horse must be trained to work with a whip on the legless side.

Russian stamp of a sidesaddle rider.

BREAKING COMPETITIONS

Various countries hold contests for breaking a horse to ride in a short period of time. One of the premier contests, the Colt Starting Challenge, is held in the United States. Four of the world's top horse whisperers are selected to break untouched horses in a three-hour time limit. At the end of the three hours, each horse and rider must negotiate an obstacle course. The winner earns $15,000 (£7,700).

🐴 Baby Long Legs

IT IS EXTREMELY DIFFICULT FOR A YOUNG FOAL TO GRAZE, BECAUSE THE LONG LEGS ARE SAID TO BE 80–90 PERCENT OF ITS ADULT LEG LENGTH, MAKING IT DIFFICULT FOR THE MOUTH TO REACH THE GROUND. COULD THIS BE NATURE'S WAY OF MAKING SURE A FOAL DOES NOT EAT TOO MUCH, TOO SOON?

To Walk or Not to Walk?

If a horse is colicking (has a stomach ache), ask your veterinarian if the horse should be made to walk until the vet arrives. Some believe this may get the horse to pass gas or resolve an impaction. The walking may also prevent the horse from lying down and rolling, which can cause serious problems with the displacement of the colon (or a significant part of the bowel), or twisting of various parts of the intestines, cutting off the blood supply to those areas, usually requiring surgery.

An Arabian foal stretching to reach the grass because of its long legs.

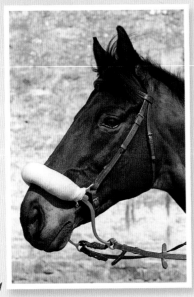

A horse wearing a mechanical hackamore.

Bitless Bridles

+ A hackamore is a type of bitless headgear consisting of a headstall, noseband, and reins. The noseband puts pressure on the horse's nose and jaw (chin area) to help the rider control the horse, instead of pressure being applied to the horse's mouth with a bit.

+ The noseband of a classic hackamore is known as a bosal. This teardrop-shaped ring is made of braided rawhide; it fits around the horse's nose, with a heel knot that rests under the horse's chin. The core of the bosal may be made of thick leather, rope, or a metal cord.

+ A bosal block is a piece of wood that is shaped like the horse's nose. It is used to shape and mold the hackamore over time, so that it will rest comfortably on the horse's nose.

+ The single-band headstall that holds the bosal is called the bosal hanger. The string-like throatlatch piece is called the fiador.

+ The reins, called the mecate, are made of horse mane or tail braided into rope, 20–25 feet (6–7.6 m) in length. The rope is tied according to a special method that allows the bosal to fit snuggly, but comfortably. The rein is one continuous loop, with a remnant piece that ties to the saddle.

+ A mechanical hackamore has a nose piece (often metal covered with leather), and metal shanks (similar to the shanks on a curb bit) extending from the nose piece, accompanied by a chain strap under the chin. These are often used on horses that do not do well with a bit in their mouths. You will occasionally see them on show jumping horses and speed event horses, such as barrel racers.

TWO OR FOUR KNEES?

★ Horses have knees on the front legs, called carpal bones. On the back legs, similarly placed joints are called hocks, not knees.

★ There are NO muscles below the knees or hocks— only ligaments, tendons, cartilage, and bone.

Front leg joints = knees

Back leg joints = hocks

CHIN UP

In all riding styles, correct head position involves keeping the chin parallel to the ground. If the rider's chin drops, the head is not centered over the body, thus affecting the proper balance of horse and rider. That is why you hear the common phrase among instructors: "Chin up!"

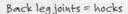

THE VAQUEROS TRADITION

The true bosal-style hackamore has a rich history with vaqueros (California reinsmen).

✳ The vaqueros base their famous training methods on dressage elements from Europe, practiced among the Moors, who passed them to the Spanish Conquistadors, who brought them to the New World.

✳ The primary vaquero objective is to train a horse without a bit to the point that it is submissive, relaxed, and responsive to all other aids (the rider's seat, voice, and legs). The horse is then introduced to a bit, often resulting in complete acceptance of the bit, with the horse being ultra-responsive and light to the rein touch.

A Spanish Mustang wearing a bosal-style hackamore and an Australian saddle.

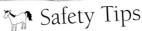 Safety Tips

Safety should be your primary concern whenever you are near a horse. The majority of horse-related accidents can be prevented, so be wise, be proactive—and be careful.

+ Don't walk up behind a horse, unless you know it sees you out of the corner of its eye. Talk as you approach the horse.

+ When walking around a tied horse, talk, put your hand on the rump, and walk close to the back legs. If you walk 4–6 feet (1–2 m) away, you may get the full impact of a kick. Ouch!

+ Don't walk under a horse's neck when directly tied to a rail or wall. It may startle the horse, while you are in a vulnerable position.

+ Lead a horse with its neck at your side. Don't walk in front of the horse where you might get pushed or stomped, or near the hip where you can easily get kicked.

+ Never stand directly in front of a horse. If it spooks, it might jump forward. Standing directly behind a horse is also a bad idea, because it puts you in position for a full-impact kick.

+ When shutting the back door or ramp of a horse trailer, always stand to the side. Unexpected backing out can be dangerous.

+ It is best to trail ride with a buddy, in case of emergencies. Always carry a cell phone, especially if you ride alone.

+ Be careful about galloping on the trails with a group of riders. Horses are herd animals, and some may panic, or get mischievous, when the group starts running.

+ When leading a horse, turn it AWAY from you to avoid having the horse step on you.

+ Never tie a horse to a piece of furniture, car bumper, or a weak fence. Unstable objects may break, or the horse may become entangled in the object.

+ Certified safety helmets (not bike helmets) are a wise thing for riders to wear, particularly inexperienced riders, jumping riders, and riders on young, inexperienced horses.

+ NEVER, NEVER, NEVER allow the horse's lead rope to be tied around your arm or waist, in case the horse spooks and runs—funerals have been held for people who have done this.

+ Always wear boots whenever working around a horse. The day you wear sandals is the day you get stepped on.

AIDS

★ Aids are tools the rider uses to control a horse.

★ Natural aids are the rider's legs, seat, hands, and voice.

★ Unnatural aids are bits, whips (bats, crops), and spurs.

Feed sweetened with molasses gives a horse extra energy.

SUGAR HIGHS

* Horses may need concentrates (grains) in addition to hay, especially if they are growing, pregnant, nursing, or working hard.

* Some concentrates, and some chopped hays, have mixed-in molasses. The feed is sometimes called a sweet feed or hot feed, because the horses tend to get high or energetic.

A horse that strains at the bit does NOT need a more severe bit, but rather to be carefully educated on how to accept the bit.

A Bit about Bits

+ The bit is a piece of material that is placed in the horse's mouth to allow the rider to control the horse. Throughout history, bits have been made of animal hide, bone, horn, wood, and metal. Today, most bits are made of metal. Stainless steel is commonly used because it is tasteless and inexpensive. Sweet iron (cold rolled steel) is popular because most horses prefer the pleasant taste. Copper is sometimes integrated into mouthpieces as a flavor enhancer, but not all horses care for it.

+ Two basic bits are the snaffle bit and the curb bit, with hundreds of variations on both styles. Most young horses have their training started in a snaffle, because it is milder. However, the mildest of bits can be severe in the wrong hands. Jerking on the reins, or heavy hands, can hurt the horse's mouth, causing much physical and mental distress to the horse.

+ Bits rest on a small gum area (the bars) of the horse's mouth, where amazingly there are no teeth. Every horse has a different-sized mouth, with the average being about 5 inches (12.5 cm) across. Bits are sold in mouthpiece size increments of a ¼ inch (6 mm) in order to find the proper size for the individual horse. A typical small-mouthed Arabian might wear a bit with a mouthpiece size of 4¾ inches (12 cm).

Bits in the Bible

"NOW IF WE PUT BITS INTO HORSES' MOUTHS TO MAKE THEM OBEY US, WE CAN GUIDE THEIR WHOLE BODIES AS WELL."

THE BIBLE, JAMES 3:3

Withering Heights

+ Horse height is measured at the middle of the withers, a bony, arched portion of the vertebrae at the neck base, leading into the back.

+ Horses are measured in units known as hands, abbreviated to h. One hand equals 4 inches (10 cm), the approximate width of a human hand.

+ Take the number of inches and divide by four (a hand). If the horse is 1 inch over 14 hands, then it is 14.1 hands tall—that is, 14 hands plus 1 inch (14.2 means 14 hands plus 2 inches; 14.3 means 14 hands plus 3 inches).

+ Generally, ponies are 14.2 hands high (hh)— 58 inches (147 cm)—or under, and horses are taller than 14.2 hh.

BEAUTIFUL LEGS

In most breeds, it is desirable to have similar front pastern and shoulder angles. The angle of the shoulder should be approximately 45 degrees to the upright, and the angle of the pastern should match. If the angles are steeper, the horse may have a restricted, choppy stride.

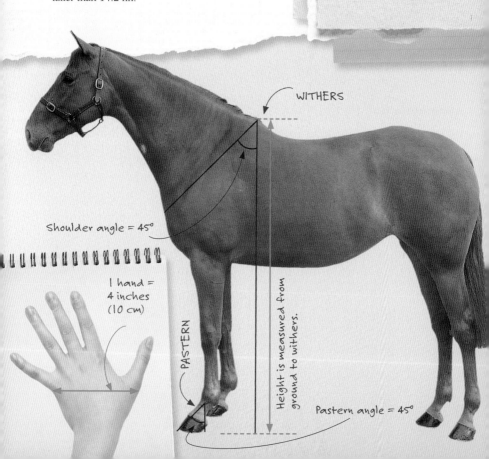

WITHERS

Shoulder angle = 45°

1 hand = 4 inches (10 cm)

PASTERN

Height is measured from ground to withers.

Pastern angle = 45°

This horse is wearing a blindfold and protective padding during a bullfight.

POLE DANCING

In Spain, a *garrocha* is a 13-foot (4-m) pole used by men on horseback to fight bulls and control herds of cattle. The poles are also incorporated into a musical dance, where the horse revolves around the pole, pivoting back and forth, and making quick, agile movements.

Raindrops Keep Falling on Their Heads

✦ *Some horses prefer to stand in the rain, snow, and hot sun, even when shelter is provided.*

✦ *It is believed that some horses naturally prefer to go out into wide open spaces, as they did prior to domestication.*

✦ *Some horses may feel safer and more comfortable outside than in unnatural, confined spaces.*

Easy Keeper

A horse that keeps good weight on limited feed and supplements is called an easy keeper.

Some horses prefer to stay outside, whatever the weather.

Unusual Gaits

The traditional four gaits are walk, trot or jog, canter or lope, and gallop, but a few breeds have different gaits. Usually smoother than the traditional gaits, these gaited horses are often recommended to riders with weak backs or poor balance. Some competitions have riders showing with a glass of champagne to demonstrate the horse's smoothness. Following are a eight popular gaited horse breeds and their unusual gaits:

❶ **The American Saddlebred** can slow gait and rack. The slow gait is a four-beat gait in which lateral legs (the legs on one side of the horse) appear to move together. The rack is a faster version where each foot hits the ground separately at equal intervals.

❷ **The Tennessee Walking Horse** can do a flat walk and running walk. The flat walk is a brisk far-reaching walk, with each foot hitting the ground separately at regular intervals. The back legs glide far forward, creating an immense overstride. The running walk is a much faster version of the gliding flat walk.

❸ **The Brazilian Mangalarga** has two unique gaits called the marcha picada and marcha batida. The marcha picada is a broken pace with very little vertical movement. The marcha batida is a diagonal four-beat gait.

❹ **The Missouri Fox Trotter** can do a fox trot, in which the front legs walk and the hindlegs trot, with a large overstride.

❺ **The Peruvian Paso** does a paso llano. This is a lateral four-beat gait where the front feet exhibit termino (rolling toward the outside, similar to a swimming motion).

❻ **The Paso Fino** has a unique gait with three speeds—classic fino, paso corto, and paso largo. The gait is a rapid four-beat lateral gait where each foot hits the ground separately at precisely equal intervals.

❼ **The Standardbred** can pace, with lateral feet stepping down in unison. It can be accomplished at slow and fast speeds.

❽ **The Icelandic Horse** can tolt; some also pace. The tolt has the same foot fall as a four-beat walk, but lacks suspension and has high knee action in the forelegs.

An Icelandic Horse performing the tolt at the Landsmot International Horse Competition in Hella, Iceland.

HIGH HEELS

✳ Unique to the Tennessee Walking Horse are high-heeled shoes called stacks. These tall shoes have stacked pads (leather or plastic) that can reach thicknesses of 4 inches (10 cm) at the heel and 2 inches (5 cm) at the toe. They are held firmly in place by a metal band.

✳ Since flat-shod Tennessee Walking Horses can perform the breed's special gaits if trained correctly, what do these high-heeled shoes accomplish? When these high stacks are added to the average horse's existing 4½-inch (11.5-cm) toe length, they result in a more dramatic, accentuated, higher lifting front leg motion for show purposes. The resulting gait, an extreme running walk, is often referred to as the "Big Lick."

The use of stacks on the Tennessee Walking Horse is controversial, with opponents citing the possibility of hoof damage.

POPULAR BREEDS FROM RUSSIA, THE BALTIC STATES, AND SCANDINAVIA

- Budyonny
- Danish Warmblood
- Dole-Gudbrandsdal
- Don
- Fjord
- Frederiksborg
- Gotland
- Icelandic Horse
- Kabardin
- Karabakh
- Knabstrup
- Latvian
- Medis Trotter
- Northlands
- Orlov Trotter
- Swedish Warmblood
- Tersky
- Ukrainian Riding Horse

THE ICELANDIC HORSE

The well-known Icelandic Horse is descended from northern Europe's Celtic Pony. The Icelandic is an extremely hardy animal, originally used for farm work, racing, and transportation. In the early part of the 20th century, they were sold to the British as pit ponies. The Icelandic is very strong and sound, quiet to handle, inquisitive, friendly, yet independent. It excels as a child's pony and as a trail mount.

Icelandic stamp featuring the Icelandic Horse.

Pit Ponies

The first record of ponies working underground in coalmines was in 1750 in Britain, where they were used to replace child and female labor for hauling coal. Numbers peaked at 70,000 in 1913. The ponies were stabled underground for 50 weeks of the year, and only brought above ground for an annual two-week vacation.

A stable down a coalmine in the United States, 1879.

🐎 Snack Time

+ Most horses love carrots, apples, sugar cubes, raisins, peppermints, grains (barley, oats, corn), molasses, apple sauce, and maple syrup.

+ Some horses are known to drink sugary soda pop from a can.

+ Never feed someone else's horse without the owner's permission, due to possible allergies and biting habits.

+ Avoid overfeeding treats, causing imbalances in nutrition.

+ Avoid feeding by hand, which can create potential nibbling and biting problems. Put the snack in the feed bin.

+ Cut up carrots and apples into small bits to avoid the risk of the horse choking.

Horses enjoy eating healthy snacks, such as apples.

Horses love sugary treats, such as sugar cubes and peppermints.

A Palomino pony enjoying a carrot snack.

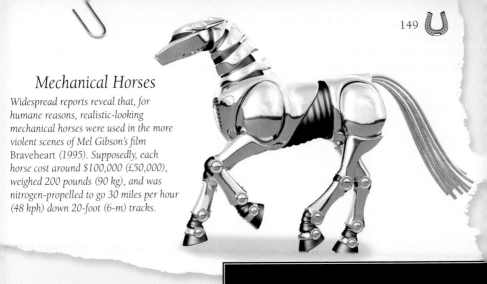

Mechanical Horses

Widespread reports reveal that, for
humane reasons, realistic-looking
mechanical horses were used in the more
violent scenes of Mel Gibson's film
Braveheart (1995). Supposedly, each
horse cost around $100,000 (£50,000),
weighed 200 pounds (90 kg), and was
nitrogen-propelled to go 30 miles per hour
(48 kph) down 20-foot (6-m) tracks.

TOP CAUSE OF HORSE DEATH
Figures indicate that colic (stomach upset,
obstructions, and spasms) is the number
one cause of horse deaths, followed by
founder as the number two cause.

A sick horse being winched into a horse
ambulance operated by the American
Society for the Prevention of Cruelty
to Animals in New York, 1888.

This Quarter Horse has a bridle path in its mane.

Help! I need air conditioning!

HORSE TACK

Horse tack comprises the equipment used to handle, ride, and drive a horse. The word tack is derived from the word tackle, as in fishing tackle or equipment. Tack stores carry an abundance of blankets, hoods, and leg and hoof boots, in every color and style imaginable. Animal prints are in this year.

Horse Haircuts

+ Some horses have a few inches of the mane behind the ears shaved off, known as a bridle path, to allow the bridle or halter to sit comfortably.

+ Many breeds have their manes shortened to a few inches by a hand-pulling and breaking process. These short manes can be braided or banded for competitions.

+ When a horse's mane is completely shaved off, it is called a roached mane. These buzz cuts are low maintenance.

+ It is not uncommon to square off the bottom of a dressage horse's tail.

+ Head-to-toe body clips can remove a winter coat. Body clips help the horse to dry faster after a sweaty workout, and look sleek and smooth in the competition arena. When not being ridden, a thick horse blanket and hood is used to keep the horse warm. If the horse gets chilled, it may start growing sporadic wiry hairs, called elephant hairs.

Antique grooming comb

Rainy Day Activity

A favorite rainy day activity among horse trainers (many of whom toil nearly seven days a week training horses) is to go shopping at tack stores for the latest horse equipment and riding fashions. When weather prohibits training, tack store businesses tend to do well.

Horse Models

Besides classifying horses as draft (heavy) horses, light horses, and ponies, horses are sometimes classified into body types related to functionality or purpose. You might equate this to cars falling into the categories of sports, sports utility, compact, subcompact, and so on. Here are a few widely used terms:

✦ **Stock horse type:** Usually refers to a strong, muscular, western-type horse used for ranching, reining, cutting, and working classes. Breed individuals that meet this criteria are often found in Quarter Horses, Mustangs, Appaloosas, and Paints.

✦ **Sport horse type:** Usually refers to an athletic horse with the substance, conformation, movement, and temperament for dressage, jumping, and eventing. Breed individuals that meet this criteria are commonly found in warmbloods, Arabians, Andalusians, Thoroughbreds, and crossbreds.

✦ **Saddle horse type:** Usually describes a more refined horse, built with an elevated front end that can be conducive to high, animated action. Breed individuals that meet this criteria are often found in Morgans, Arabians, Saddlebreds, Tennessee Walkers, and Hackneys.

The saddle-horse-type Morgan is a favorite all-round family horse. It stretches out its hindlegs to make mounting easier.

SHOED OR SHOD?

- It is correct to say, "My horse is getting shoes."
- It is correct to say, "My horse is getting shod."
- It is incorrect to say, "My horse is getting shoed."

WHAT A STRETCH

✦ *Some saddle-horse types, such as South African Saddlebreds, American Saddlebreds, Hackneys, and Morgans, are taught to park out (stretch) their bodies for the low, easy mounting and dismounting of the rider.*

✦ *Male horses stretch out all four legs (like a rocking horse) in order to urinate without getting their legs wet.*

BIG BELLIES Hay bellies in horses are likened to beer bellies in people.

Cookies! Chocolate!

HORSE COOKIES

YOU WILL NEED:

1 cup uncooked oats
1 cup flour
1 cup shredded carrots
1 teaspoon salt
1 teaspoon sugar
2 teaspoons vegetable oil
¼ cup molasses

Mix all the ingredients together in a bowl. Form the mixture into small balls and place them on a greased cookie sheet. Bake at 350°F (175°C) for 15 minutes, or until golden brown.

Tip: Vary the ingredients with some of the horse's favorite treats, such as other grains, apples, peppermints, raisins, or maple syrup.

CURB THE CHOCOLATE Chocolate is banned for racehorses because it contains a potent stimulant, theobromine, and small amounts of caffeine.

Mutton Withers

A horse should have prominent withers to allow the saddle to stay secure and not slide. Saddles slip on horses with mutton withers (flat, broad withers, common in fat horses and ponies), but mutton withers are more comfortable for bareback riders.

Horse Vision

- A horse's eyes are set on the side of the head, allowing it to see two different pictures, one with each eye. The sightline of the eyes can converge straight ahead to focus on one object. This area of convergence is the only area where the horse can clearly judge distances.

- Horses' side-set eyes and flexible necks are well suited for grazing. The field of vision is wide, with limited blind spots, so potential predators can be sighted.

- Studies indicate that horses have dichromatic vision, allowing them to see a limited range of colors, usually the ones found in nature.

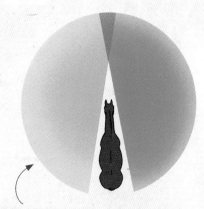

A horse sees a different picture with each eye. The V-shaped area in front of its head can be seen with both eyes.

HORSE SPECTRUM

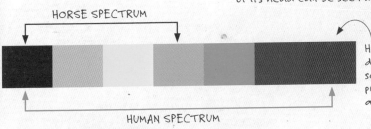

HUMAN SPECTRUM

Horses have difficulty seeing blue, purple, and violet.

Diamonds are a horsewoman's second best friend—her horse is number one.

ANNIVERSARY GIFTS FOR THAT SPECIAL HORSEWOMAN

Year	Traditional gift	Horsewoman's gift
One	Paper gift	Subscription to horse magazine
Five	Silverware	Saddle with silver nameplate
Ten	Diamond	Riding blouse pin with diamond
Fifteen	Crystal	New truck
Twenty	Platinum	High-quality show horse
Thirty	Diamond	New barn
Forty	Ruby	New hip
Fifty	Gold	Back brace
Sixty	Diamond	Diamond

THE FAR SIDE

Most riders tack up and mount their horses from the near side—the left side.

* Traditionally, horses are mounted, lead, and tacked up (fitted with saddle and bridle) at their left side, called the near side. Most riders are right-handed, making it awkward to use the right side (far side).

* Another popular explanation is that the near side was used by military riders who had swords attached to the left side of their bodies. By mounting on the horse's left side, the sword did not interfere with the mounting process.

Horse Heaters

+ The average-sized horse produces about 38,000 kilojoules of heat daily; therefore, when they are in barns, the need for ventilation is important.

+ In colder climates, many barns are heated by machines, supplemented by the body heat of the horses.

+ Horses huddle up in the snow to form their own heating unit.

Horses stay together to keep warm.

Branding: Ouch!

+ Branding is used for identification purposes. Identifying ownership by branding dates back to ancient Egyptian times.

+ Hot-iron branding is still performed on some horse breeds, as with cattle. Usually, brands depict the ranch name, or the lineage of the horse.

+ Freeze branding with liquid nitrogen is considered more humane, causing the hair to turn white on the branded area.

+ The Jockey Club (the international organization for registering Thoroughbreds) requires tattoos on the upper lips of racehorses.

+ Microchips are implanted into the necks of many breeds.

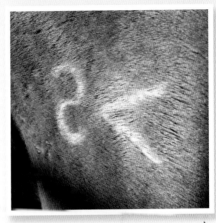

A freeze brand causes the branded area of hair to turn white.

Sample Brands
Many horse breeds have a breed society brand.
Here are a few of the more common ones:

AMERICAN WARMBLOOD

BRITISH WARMBLOOD

DANISH WARMBLOOD

SWEDISH WARMBLOOD

DUTCH WARMBLOOD

SWISS WARMBLOOD

AUSTRALIAN WARMBLOOD

NEW ZEALAND WARMBLOOD

SELLE FRANÇAIS

OLDENBURG

HANOVERIAN

HOLSTEINER

TRAKEHNER

RHEINLAND

WESTPHALIEN

A galloping herd of horses, displaying their flight instinct.

Herd Behavior

+ Horses are prey animals with the flight or fight instinct.

+ Herds have a dominant leader (usually an older, experienced alpha mare) who makes critical choices for the herd's safety (for example, the safest routes to take).

+ Stallions have been observed to "own" a herd and run behind it to make sure that slower horses catch up, and to separate the herd from predators.

+ A management firm studied equine herd behavior and noticed dynamics that parallel effective management—an experienced leader who has the welfare of the group in mind; a group that sticks together through thick and thin; and members watching over the needs of each other (such as standing over a sleeping horse).

SPOOKING HORSES

Some horses spook more than others, and certain breeds are known to be more timid and cowardly than other breeds. Some horses spook because they were previously punished for being afraid of something (water, a bike, a dog). Some horses spook because of circumstances or features that resemble those in previous accidents. Poor eyesight may also cause spookiness. When carrying a rider, horses tend to have a pattern in which they spook:

* Some stop dead in their tracks and stare at the frightening object.

* Some jump to the side, or make a quick 180-degree turn.

* Some take off running, as they would in the wild as flight animals.

Molly the pony, with her prosthetic limb.

Three-legged Horses

Some three-legged horses have survived. Molly, a gray-speckled Pony of the Americas, was stranded in a Louisiana barn during Hurricane Katrina in 2005. After being taken to a rescue farm, her leg became infected after a pitbull dog attacked her. She was eventually fitted with a prosthetic limb, with a "happy face" on the base so that she would leave its imprint when she walked. After her recovery, Molly was taken to visit shelters, hospitals, nursing homes, and rehabilitation centers, bringing hope and inspiration to the human occupants. *Molly the Pony*, a children's book by Pam Kaster, tells Molly's story.

Horses in Rehab

Yes, there are rehab centers for horses. Rehabilitation centers are also known as lay-up facilities. Horses are usually sent there for specialized medical treatment and recuperation from injuries and surgeries. These facilities are common for racehorses, for whom the chances of injury are much higher than for non-racing horses.

Talking Tails

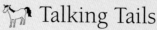

Just as a horse's ears and body language communicate messages, tails do the same.

+ A flagged tail, where the horse waves its tail like a flag, usually means excitement leading to explosive behavior. The horse may be preparing to flee.

+ Stallions often flag their tails after sexual intercourse. Mares often raise their tails when they are in heat.

+ A tail tucked down and clamped to the body may indicate fear or fright.

+ An aggressively swishing tail or a wringing tail (where the tail can rotate like a propeller in a circular motion) may mean anger, frustration, or resentment.

+ A mildly swishing tail may mean the horse is attempting to bat off flies and insects.

An Arabian stallion flags its tail in excitement as it trots around its paddock.

Lotsa Road Apples

A mature horse eats about seven times its weight each year.

Horses often swish their tails while grazing to deter insects.

> I prefer to describe myself as "exotic."

Grade Horses

HAVE YOU HEARD OF A MONGREL DOG BEING CALLED A HEINZ 57 OR A MUTT? WELL, THE HORSE VERSION OF AN INDIVIDUAL WITHOUT KNOWN HERITAGE IS A GRADE HORSE.

HALVES AND QUARTERS

Appendix Quarter Horses are half-Thoroughbred and half-Quarter Horse, and are sometimes called Racing Quarter Horses.

 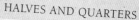

THEY SHOOT HORSES, DON'T THEY?

* They Shoot Horses, Don't They?, the 1969 Academy Award-winning movie, had nothing to do with horses. The movie was about a marathon dance contest during the Depression of the 1930s, with poverty-stricken participants struggling to keep dancing in order to win a cash prize. Historically, horses were often shot to be put out of pain quickly, especially in the case of a broken leg. The movie title is commenting on the fact that human beings are expected to endure great pain, while animals are not.

* Today, a horse with a serious broken leg is likely to be euthanized. Horses do not wear casts well, and they must move to keep their circulation going. Lack of movement can result in pneumonia or laminitis (a crippling inflammation of the foot caused by poor circulation). Once a broken leg heals, the horse might not move correctly, and its usefulness may be forfeited.

* Barbaro, the 2006 Kentucky Derby winner, was euthanized after breaking his leg and struggling for more than eight months with treatment complications.

Nowadays, horses are humanely euthanized by barbiturate overdose—"put to sleep"—not shot.

🐎 Horseshoes

+ Shoes are put on horses to prevent the feet from chipping under heavy use. Shoes also help to maintain the shape of the feet for maximum performance.

+ Horseshoes are usually made out of various metals, including iron, titanium, and aluminum. New innovations include glue-on shoes and cushioned rubber shoes.

+ Borium shoes with added traction are used on parade horses so that they will not slip on streets. Spiked shoes, such as cleats, are often put on horses that run or jump on slick grass.

+ Most horses require new shoes every 6–8 weeks, although some breeds, like Saddlebreds, Arabians, Morgans, and Hackneys, can wait a few weeks more, thus creating higher leg action.

+ In the wild, the horn of the horse's hoof toughens and breaks off naturally, and wears down. Depending on their use, some horses can go barefoot with trims (just like toenail trims) about every 6–8 weeks.

+ Hooves are thought to grow ⅜ inch (1 cm) per month, and can grow out from the coronet band to the ground in a period of a year.

+ Artists and welders turn used shoes into wreaths, Christmas trees, sculptures, hat racks, furniture, toilet paper dispensers, and so on.

THINGS NAMED AFTER HORSESHOES
• Horseshoe crab
• Horseshoe Falls, Niagara River, Canada
• Horseshoe bats
• Horseshoe worm (Phylum Phoronida)

The horseshoe bat is named because of the horseshoe-shaped flap of skin on its nose.

The horseshoe crab is named because of the shape of its shell.

Allow a weaving horse to see other animals from its stall.

Worrisome Weaving

✦ Horses that are bored, lonely, or anxious may develop a vice called weaving. In a stall, weaving horses will continuously rock, swaying their necks side to side, or up and down. When these horses are placed in areas larger than box stalls, they may also pace back and forth.

✦ Weight loss and joint problems can result from weaving.

✦ There are several ways to tackle the problem: provide a companion animal, such as a goat or donkey; make other horses visible from the stall; or place a large mirror across from the stall so that the horse becomes its own security.

Use a mirror to "create" horse companions.

A Clydesdale and donkey snuggle together in friendly companionship.

Antique embroidered wall hanging of a horse drinking.

"You Can Lead a Horse to Water, But You Can't Make It Drink"

This well-known saying often serves as an analogy for human behavior. Someone may be provided with an opportunity (job, help, responsibility, advice), but that person must make a choice whether or not to accept the opportunity.

Trick Horses

In circuses and exhibitions throughout the world, horses are trained to perform some amazing feats, such as jumping over an automobile, jumping through a hoop of fire, walking a narrow plank, sitting down, laying down, playing dead, bowing down, rearing, rearing and walking at the same time, pushing a baby stroller, picking up or pushing objects, counting with their front legs, smiling, kissing, hugging, rolling over, and so on. This is a testament to the heart of a horse to please humankind.

This Appaloosa has been taught to bow down and poke out its tongue.

Saddled horses having a lunch break from trail riding.

Cold-backed Horses

◆ Occasionally, a horse may act cold-backed when a rider mounts it. Symptoms include the horse dipping away or raising its back, and even an unexpected rodeo where the horse attempts to get rid of the rider.

◆ Some horses may just tighten their back muscles and refuse to move forward, and when they do move forward, it may take a few minutes for the horse to relax its mind and muscles.

◆ Cold-backed reactions may be caused by various factors, including soreness in the back, nervousness about handling a rider, or in anticipation of getting pinched when the saddle moves.

◆ Just like people, some horses need to do stretching exercises before they begin their workouts. That is why a horseman might lunge a horse on a line, or hand walk it for a few minutes prior to mounting.

◆ On most mounted horses, it is common practice to allow the horse to walk, stretch, loosen, and relax for approximately 5–10 minutes prior to commencing the riding session.

SUPPLEMENTS GALORE

Horses, just like humans, have health food stores with every imaginable product on the shelf. Where do you begin? It is a complex science deciding how to balance the horse's need for over 15 different minerals, in addition to other trace minerals (those needed in smaller amounts). Veterinarians and certified horse nutritionists are your best bet for making these decisions.

A tense horse tries to buck the rider off its back.

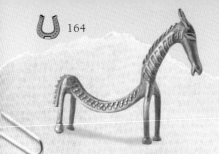

Sway-backed pony

SWAY-BACKED HORSES

A sway back is also called lordosis or hollow back. The condition makes it difficult to train a horse to round its spine properly in a supple, athletic manner, which is essential for performing high-level maneuvers. It is thought to be caused by one or more of the following factors:

* From riding a horse when it is too young and lacks the musculature and strength to hold a rider.

* From carrying a heavy rider for long periods of time.

* From being pregnant many times.

* From old age accompanied by the weakening of the muscles and ligaments.

ROACH-BACKED HORSES

The opposite of a sway back is a roach back, where the back resembles the back of a pig. This conformation trait is not very common, but when it exists, it is usually accompanied by a steep shoulder angle and rough gaits.

Natural Horsemanship

+ Sound training and riding principles used throughout the ages are now being marketed in the form of natural horsemanship, where special attention is given to natural instincts and behaviors of horses in the wild.

+ The methods are considered non-violent, starting with relationship-building exercises on the ground. The horse is gradually accustomed to the application and release of pressure. Over time, as confidence develops, newer concepts are introduced until the horse is rideable. The philosophy and methods permeate every aspect of training as the horse ages.

+ The ancient Greek soldier and historian Xenephon (430–355 B.C.) was one of the first people to advocate training the horse through sympathetic methods using the understanding of natural instincts and building relationships.

Xenephon

Horses travel cargo-class.

Air Transportation

✳ Horses are transported by most modes of transportation, including airplanes.

✳ Horses are put into a comfortable metal container that goes in the cargo section of the plane.

✳ A qualified horse attendant usually stays near the horse throughout the flight.

✳ International flights usually require horse passports, extensive vaccinations, and a 30-day quarantine before, and sometimes after, flight.

✳ Up to 70 horses can be flown in one DC-10 airplane.

🐎 Growing Upward

✦ A common thought is that, at birth, foals are at least 60 percent of their final height.

✦ Most horse breeds are said to reach somewhere between 80 and 95 percent of their height by 24 months of age, and yet continue marginal growth into their fifth and sixth years. Some breeds have been known to gain height in their seventh year.

✦ It is important to many horsemen to have a tall adult horse. A common belief, which would be difficult to prove, is that a horse castrated at an early age (as soon as the testicles descend) may ultimately end up taller than if the horse were gelded later (aged two or older).

Mares with their foals of different ages and heights.

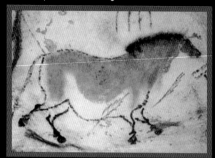

Lascaux cave painting of a horse.

Horses in Art

✦ Horses have been depicted in art since prehistoric times. The images of horses found in the famous Lascaux cave paintings in southwestern France date back 16,000 years.

✦ George Stubbs (1724–1806), one of the greatest equestrian painters, earned the label "Mr. Stubbs the horse painter" in his own lifetime. He brought a new dimension to animal art with his natural and anatomically accurate depictions—he dissected horse carcasses and had engravings made of his studies to help him.

✦ Despite his anatomical knowledge, even Stubbs was unable to depict a fast-moving horse realistically. Those artists who did try to depict a galloping horse tended to portray them with all four legs outstretched— an impossibility. It was not until the freeze-action photographic studies of animal motion by Eadweard Muybridge (1830–1904) that artists began to understand horse gaits and how to represent them.

"Horse Attacked by a Lion" by George Stubbs, 1769.

Sequential galloping horse by Eadweard Muybridge.

"Cholo," an intimate portrait of an Azteca wearing a traditional Mexican headstall—painting by contemporary artist Shannon Lawlor.

Bridleless Horses

THE BRIDLE IS THE PIECE OF EQUIPMENT THAT FITS OVER THE HORSE'S HEAD, STABILIZES THE BIT IN THE HORSE'S MOUTH, AND IS USED TO CONTROL THE HORSE. HORSES THAT ARE HIGHLY TRAINED TO WORK OFF THE RIDER'S SEAT, LEGS, AND VOICE CAN SOMETIMES BE RIDDEN WITHOUT A BRIDLE. JUMPING COURSES AND REINING PATTERNS HAVE BEEN PERFORMED BRIDLELESS IN SPECIAL COMPETITIONS.

Jumping Records

♦ Horses have been known to break high jumping records of over 8 feet (2.4 m), and there are unofficial reports of a horse jumping 8 feet 3½ inches (252.7 cm).

♦ Reportedly, one of the longest jumps ever made by a horse was 27 feet 6¾ inches (840.1 cm).

Germany and the U.S. dominate Olympic equestrian events.

FÉDÉRATION EQUESTRE INTERNATIONALE

☆ Founded in 1921, the Fédération Equestre Internationale (F.E.I.) is recognized by the International Olympic Committee (I.O.C.) as the international body governing equestrian sport. There are 135 affiliated national federations within the F.E.I.

☆ The F.E.I. is the sole authority for regulations and approval for international events (including the Olympic Games) in dressage, jumping, eventing, driving, endurance, vaulting, reining, and para-equestrian (riders with physical disabilities).

☆ In 2006, France was the country that organized the greatest number of competitions (249), followed by Germany (179), and the United States (162).

☆ Jumping is the F.E.I.'s largest discipline for number of events, followed in order by eventing, endurance, dressage, driving, reining, vaulting, and para-equestrian.

☆ The F.E.I. takes a strong stand on the humane treatment of horses and has a code of conduct that reads:
"At all stages during the preparation and training of competition horses, welfare must take precedence over all other demands."

OLYMPIC EVENTS

✻ Olympic show jumping has been dominated by Germany. The nation has won 13 gold medals, more than any other country.

✻ Germany has more team dressage medals than any other country (18 golds, 7 silvers, and 7 bronzes).

✻ Olympic three-day eventing has traditionally been dominated by the United States.

Gold-medal show
jumping winner
Meredith Michaels-
Beerbaum on
Shutterfly at the
2007 F.E.I. European
Championships
in Mannheim, Germany.

A medieval knight with a lance.

Jousting Knights

✦ The medieval knight was an elite mounted warrior sworn to uphold the code of chivalry, which promoted the values of faith, loyalty, courage, courtesy, compassion, and honor.

✦ Jousting tournaments became a popular entertainment, with two mounted knights competing to display their combat skills and win a fortune in prize money. The knights would charge, or tilt, at each other with a lance, trying to unhorse their opponent with it.

✦ King Henry II of France died at the age of 40 when a shard of his opponent's broken lance penetrated his visor, pierced his eye, and came out through his ear.

✦ Modern-day jousting or tilting takes place under the auspices of the International Jousting Association, using breakable lance tips for safety.

A modern-day jousting tournament.

EWE-NECKED HORSES

A conformation fault known as an upside-down neck or ewe neck occurs when the arched shape and muscling is more developed on the underside of the neck. This fault can make it difficult for the horse to breathe when the rider attempts to get the horse to collect (lowering the hindquarters, arching the spine, and elevating the front end to provide for a soft, comfortable ride).

A Mangalarga with a ewe neck.

How to Tie a Slipknot

For safety purposes, the standard knot for tying a horse to an object is the quick-release slipknot. You want to be able to release a tied horse quickly if it panics, falls, or gets hung up on something. Study the picture below and practice on a broomstick or pole that will simulate a hitching rail. Notice that you push through a doubled portion, allowing the loose end to be pulled for a quick release.

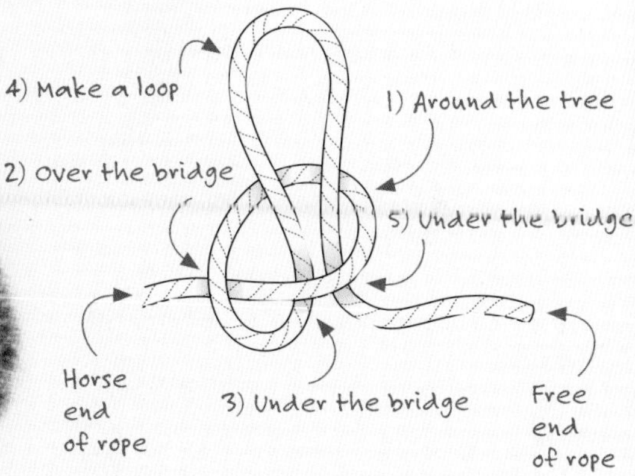

4) Make a loop

1) Around the tree

2) Over the bridge

5) Under the bridge

Horse end of rope

3) Under the bridge

Free end of rope

REMEMBER THE SQUIRREL'S JOURNEY

Some people come up with clever ways to remember how to tie a slipknot, such as:

"The squirrel's path went around the tree (the pole to which you are tying), then over and under the bridge, made a loop, and came back under the bridge."

COMMON NAMES
FOR HORSE MANURE
• Meadow muffins
• Road apples
• Horse balls
• Alley apples
  (urban horse deposits)
• Free souvenirs
• Horse hockey
• Horse biscuits

BREECHES OR BRITCHES?

The term breeches is a plural noun (similar to scissors vs. scissor) that refers to jodhpurs—a wide-hipped English riding pant that tightens around the knees and ankles in order that a tall boot may fit over the legs. The term britches is just an alteration of the word, and is often used interchangeably with breeches. Britches means pants.

Some people clean the Curly Horse's winter coat by vacuuming it.

Curly Horses

✦ The Curly Horse, also known as the Bashkir, is considered to be hypoallergenic, having a unique protein structure in the curly hair. Most people who are allergic to horses have a reduced or no allergic reaction to Curlies.

✦ Native Americans considered them sacred, and called them buffalo ponies.

HAIRLESS HORSES

Reports exist of rare, hairless horses in circuses. Historically, some Belgian Draft foals have been born hairless from a terminal skin disease called junctional epidermolysis bullosa.

CLEVER HANS

In 1888 in Germany, Wilhelm von Osten trained a horse in basic arithmetic. Clever Hans became famous the world over for his counting skills, tapping out with his hoof mostly correct answers to basic counting questions. The horse was estimated to have the mathematical ability of a 14-year-old child. However, in 1907 it was proved that Hans was responding not to the questions, but to almost imperceptible visual cues in his human observers.

BREEDING STALLIONS

✳ Stallions can be bred to mares via live cover, or they can be pasture bred. With live cover, the mare is presented to the stallion in the breeding shed when she is ready to mate. The stallion then physically "covers" the mare. A team of handlers is usually present so that the horses can be separated should there be any trouble. When pasture bred, the stallion is let loose with the mare in a pasture to breed naturally.

✳ Artificial insemination (A.I.) is now quite common. The stallion's sperm is collected in a lab, where it is cooled or frozen, and then shipped to the mare for insemination. How romantic.

✳ A stallion with a curled up lip may be expressing sexual excitement.

Clever Hans performing.

Standardbreds in a harness race.

THEY'RE OFF AND RUNNING

☆ Horse racing, one of the world's most popular spectator sports, is called the sport of kings. It was originally enjoyed by 17th-century royalty.

☆ Thoroughbreds hold the world records for running long distances at the fastest speeds.

☆ Quarter Horses are bred to excel in short, ¼-mile (400-m) races.

☆ Standardbred horses pull two-wheeled carts (sulkies) in trotting or pacing races, called harness races.

Chariot Racing

+ A chariot is an early type of carriage, usually formed from a floor with raised sides to protect the charioteer. Drawn by two or more horses, chariots were used in ancient times by the Assyrians, Babylonians, Egyptians, Indians, Greeks, Romans, and others.

+ Chariots were used in battle, but also for travel, processions, and games and races. The racing of chariots became a popular Roman and Greek sport.

+ In 680 B.C., chariot racing was introduced to the Olympics. In Olympia, on a track called the Hippodrome, up to 60 chariots raced at one time. Some races were for two-horse chariots, and some were for four-horse chariots. Drivers were selected similar to the way jockeys are chosen today, based on their light weight.

+ For the movie *Ben Hur* (1959), featuring a spectacular chariot race that took over three months to complete, the trainer was said to have trained the horses in Italy for 11 months prior to filming. He taught each horse individually, then in pairs, and then in threes and fours. There were nine chariot teams and 72 horses trained (36 actually made it).

Ancient Egyptian relief of a two-horse chariot.

Quadrilles

★ A quadrille is a group of four horses and riders that executes a series of movements in synchronization. The kaleidoscope effect of weaving these intricate patterns is an entertaining representation of horsemanship at its finest. Usually choreographed to music, the riders and horses perform in matching tack and attire.

★ The quadrille was performed in the Baroque era, especially in schools of equitation such as the Spanish Riding School. Today, the quadrille is recognized as a competitive event.

The popularity of horse quadrilles led to the creation of the quadrille dance in the 18th century, performed by four couples.

DRILL TEAMS

The equestrian drill team is a variation of the Spanish Riding School's quadrille. Throughout the world, drill teams can take on many different styles and purposes. Usually performing for exhibition in rodeos and parades, these matching groups can contain large numbers (double digits) of horses and riders. Just like in the quadrille, the group performs intricate patterns at various speeds, producing a kaleidoscope effect. Some groups use a specific breed or color of horse. Some ride side saddle. Some do fast, trick riding, whereas others may perform classical dressage movements.

A display by the mounted soldiers of the Cuadro Verde of Chile.

DO I LOOK FAT?

Here is how to "guestimate" a horse's weight:

❋ Measure the horse's length, in inches, in a straight line from where the shoulder meets the chest to the back of the hindquarters.

❋ Measure the circumference, in inches, of the heart girth (behind the elbow) using a cloth tape measure.

❋ Use this formula:
Heart girth x heart girth x length/300 + 50 = horse's approximate weight in pounds

❋ To calculate the weight in metric, take the measurements in centimeters and then use this formula:
Heart girth x heart girth x length/11,900 = horse's approximate weight in kilograms

❋ Tack stores sell weight-measuring tapes that are put around the heart girth to make an estimate. Apparently, they are very inaccurate for high-withered horses, foals, and Miniature Horses.

Buckskins

❋ A Buckskin horse has a color resembling tanned deer hide, with black legs, and a black mane and tail.

❋ Duns are a duller colored version of the Buckskin, carrying the dun-factor gene that often results in a dorsal stripe, shoulder striping, and zebra markings on the upper legs.

❋ A brindle dun, which actually has the coloring of a brindle dog—that is, the dun coloration with additional dark streaks or flecks—exists in horses that are native to the Netherlands.

❋ Famous Buckskins include Buttermilk, the horse of Roy Rogers' wife Dale Evans; the horse ridden by Ben Cartwright in the TV show *Bonanza*, called Buck; and Spirit, from the 2002 animated movie *Spirit: Stallion of the Cimarron*.

A Buckskin Mustang

To "guestimate" a horse's weight, measure length,...

...then measure heart girth (all the way around).

Top Heavy

Most horses are known to carry 65 percent of their body weight on their forelimbs. Training and conditioning help to engage the hindquarters and elevate the forehand (the front half of the horse's body), allowing for greater agility and balance.

The Budweiser Clydesdales at a World Series baseball game in St. Louis, Missouri.

🐎 Brewery Horses

Although a draft horse is any type of horse used to pull any type of vehicle, it is usually associated with heavy breeds.

✦ Originally bred for the purposes of heavy farm work and haulage, draft horses have become a well-loved sight transporting drays of beer barrels in many towns and cities around the world. Brewery horses often wear custom-made brass and patent leather harnesses that can weigh 175 pounds (80 kg).

✦ The Shire Horse of England is the breed that is best known to produce the largest horses in the world. Shire Horses can reach over 18 hands high—72 inches (183 cm)—and weigh just over a ton. Some brewery Shire Horses were given a daily allowance of a bucket of beer—with each horse making its preference known.

✦ The Anheuser Busch Brewery's "Budweiser Clydesdales" have celebrity status in the United States, with hitch teams touring the country, and plans to go international. The 2008 Super Bowl commercial starring a Clydesdale horse and a Dalmatian dog was ranked as the coveted number one commercial for the $2.6 million (£1.3 million) 30-second time slot.

Horse brasses are collector's items.

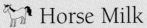 Horse Milk

**Horse milk is consumed among humans in many countries around the world.
The taste is said to be mild, light, and sweeter than cow's milk.**

+ Horse milk is considered a rich source of vitamins and minerals that is easily digested, with 1.5 percent fat compared to cow's milk at 3.7 percent.

+ Horse milk has been touted as an effective 28-day internal cleanser that boosts the immune system and energy level. It can have a laxative effect.

+ Amish farmers in the United States are avid producers of horse milk.

+ Horse milk was popular in Germany during World War I, and is now consumed as a delicacy and health product in some parts of western Europe.

+ Kumis is a popular Mongolian drink, containing a mild amount of alcohol made from fermented mare's milk.

+ Belgian Draft Horses and Haflingers are two breeds that farmers use to produce milk. There is even a Belgian Horse Milk Dairy Association that regulates the quality of the milk.

+ Horse milk products can include yogurt, ice cream, and liquor (similar to wine).

+ Milking a horse can be somewhat dangerous, with the attendants having to reach up high between agile legs that can kick.

+ A typical milking day involves five milkings at 2½-hour intervals, yielding only ½–1 pint (¼–½ l) of milk per session. This makes for an expensive delicacy.

The Belgian Draft Horse is a popular breed for producing milk for human consumption.

THE BANDANA

The cowboy kerchief (bandana) had many uses, most notably as a dust mask, as earmuffs for cold weather, as protection from the sun, as a pot holder, as a tourniquet, and as a blindfold for animals. Unfortunately, it was also used as a mask while robbing stagecoaches. It was generally folded into a triangle and tied around the neck with the knot in the back.

A bandana is a multitasking accessory.

Horses communicate using snorts, squeals, and neighs.

THE TALKING HORSE

Besides body, ear, and tail language, horses also communicate with sounds.

+ A loud, snorting or blowing sound usually alerts other horses to the possibility of danger.

+ A squeal or scream usually indicates that a horse is preparing to fight or defend itself.

+ A neigh or whinny is a loud, commonly used sound for a horse to announce its presence, or call out for another horse.

+ A nicker is a subtle, quiet sound that often expresses fondness for another horse or humans.

Horses and Water

* Horses tend to colic (get stomach aches) more in winter, when they drink less water and there is often less moisture in the aged, stored winter hay.

* Some horsemen break their young horses in lakes or oceans to limit potential bucking and rearing.

* Domesticated horses often drink out of automatic water fountains, which they push on with their nose.

* A horse can secrete up to 10 gallons (38 l) of saliva per day.

HOW MUCH WATER DOES A HORSE NEED?

Provide 1 gallon (3.8 l) of water per 100 pounds (45 kg) of body weight per day.

Foal's First Feeding

Ideally, foals should stand up and nurse within an hour. The first milk contains the all-important colostrum (often referred to as colostrums) that contains the antibodies the foal needs to build its immunity system.

MAKE A BIRTHDAY CAKE FOR YOUR HORSE

YOU WILL NEED:

4 cups sweet feed (finely chopped hay mixed with molasses)
1 cup molasses or honey
1 apple, sliced

Mix the ingredients, and mold into a cake shape. Add icing made from granulated sugar and a small amount of water. Decorate with candles made from carrot sticks.

A mare feeding her foal while grazing.

Horse Statue Myth

Folk wisdom has it that equestrian statues contain a code whereby the rider's fate can be determined by noting how many hooves the horse has raised. The most common theory is that if one hoof is raised, the rider was wounded in battle (possibly dying of those wounds later but not necessarily so); two raised hooves mean the rider died in battle; all four hooves on the ground mean the rider survived all battles unharmed.

Two raised hooves indicate that this rider died in battle.

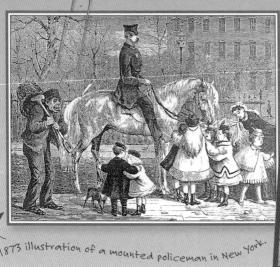

1873 illustration of a mounted policeman in New York.

Mounted police officers are a popular sight all over the world.

🐎 Ten-Foot Cops

The ability of a horse to negotiate the terrain of modern cities makes the animal an important part of a security team. Mounted police are used in many situations, from patrolling malls and music concerts to parks and riots.

✦ Mounted police are often known as 10-foot cops, because they are so high off the ground, making them visible from a block away. The height gives the officers a huge advantage in large crowds.

✦ Police horses must go through rigorous training to desensitize them to noises and frightening objects. It is not uncommon for the horses to be trained to accept loud vehicles, smoke, flares, gun shots, a 6-foot (2-m) ball, water puddles, trash piles, and waving flags.

✦ There are dangers to the horse in this line of service. It is not uncommon for police horses to be attacked by dogs, or injured by criminals. A mounted police horse in Hyderabad, India, was frightened in a riot. The horse slipped, hit its head on a boulder, and died instantly.

✦ Special horseshoes (often made from borium or rubber) help to prevent the horses from slipping on the streets.

✦ The New York Police Department has access to approximately 90 horses that are used to patrol the streets and parks of Manhattan.

✦ The Royal Canadian Mounted Police are part of a 100-year mounted police tradition. Sometimes called the "Red Police," their riding attire is primarily comprised of the color red.

✦ The mounted officers of the Red Guard of Senegal pride themselves on superior horsemanship skills, often competing in races, show jumping, and steeple chasing.

✦ Mounted police, called Carabinieri, are skilled riders who help protect the people of Italy.

✦ Over 200 horses are housed by the Guards of Paris, a mounted cavalry unit.

AGE CALCULATOR

You can make a rough conversion of a horse's age to human years by using the formula of multiplying the known age by 2.2.

Example: 20-year-old horse x 2.2 = 44 years in human terms

Another age calculation sometimes used is counting the horse's first year equal to ten human years, and every year after that as two human years.

Example: 20-year-old horse = (1 x 10) + (19 x 2) = 48 years in human terms

How to Hand Feed

Be careful. Horses have powerful bites that could easily sever a finger. Do not hand feed an unfamiliar or irritable horse.

Time for a snack!

* Cut an apple or carrot into slices, and put one piece on your hand. Spread your hand out flat, palm up. Do not let your fingertips roll up. It is best if you arch your palm slightly backward, with your fingertips bent toward the ground.
* Some horses get mouthy and start a biting habit when fed by hand.

Sea Horses

SOME HORSES ACTUALLY ENJOY OCEAN SWIMMING. SOMETIMES, IF THEY HAVE NEVER BEEN IN THE WATER BEFORE, THEY MAY BE AFRAID, BUT THEY ARE EASILY TRAINED TO GET OVER THEIR INITIAL FEAR. THEY DO NOT HAVE TO BE TAUGHT TO SWIM—THEY KNOW HOW ALREADY. HOWEVER, WHEN SWIMMING A HORSE FOR THE FIRST TIME, GIVE IT EXTRA ATTENTION, BECAUSE SOME HORSES HAVE BEEN KNOWN TO SINK.

🐎 Popcorn and a Movie

A great idea for horse-themed parties, get-togethers, or riding camps is to show a horse-themed movie. Following is a list of some of the all-time great horse movies:

+ *Black Beauty* (1921, 1946, 1971, 1994), all based on Anna Sewell's classic book of 1877.

+ *A Day At the Races* (1937), a Marx Brothers comedy about horse racing.

+ *The Long Shot* (1939), a lighthearted film about horse racing.

+ *My Friend Flicka* (1943), based on Mary O'Hara's novel and starring Roddy McDowall.

+ *National Velvet* (1944), about the girl who rode in the Grand National steeplechase, starring Elizabeth Taylor.

+ *Thunderhead, Son of Flicka* (1945), based on the Mary O'Hara novel.

+ *Green Grass of Wyoming* (1948), based on the Mary O'Hara novel.

+ *The Story of Seabiscuit* (1949), about the famous Thoroughbred racehorse.

+ *The Red Pony* (1949, 1973), both adaptations of the 1933 John Steinbeck classic novella.

+ *Francis the Talking Mule* series of seven comedies (1950s), about a talking army mule.

+ *Outlaw Stallion* (1954), about a horse rustler and a wild white stallion.

+ *The Gypsy Colt* (1954), about a horse that journeys 500 miles (800 km) to reunite with its owner.

+ *Misty* (1961), about a pony on Chincoteague Island.

+ *The Horsemasters* (1961), about equestrians trying to get certified by the British Horse Society.

+ *Miracle of the White Stallions* (1963), about the Lipizzaners of the Spanish Riding School during World War II.

NATIONAL VELVET
In the motion picture "National Velvet," starring Elizabeth Taylor, the starring horse was named The Pie. His real name was King Charles. The seven-year-old Thoroughbred was the grandson of the famed racehorse Man O' War.

King Charles also starred in "The Harvey Girls" in 1945.

The head of Black Stallion, from the 1979 movie poster.

+ *The Horse in the Gray Flannel Suit* (1968), a Disney comedy about a show horse.

+ *Blue Fire Lady* (1977), about a strained father/daughter relationship, centered around her love for horses.

+ *Danny* (1977), about a young girl and a pony she rehabilitates to show victory.

+ *International Velvet* (1978), a spin-off of *National Velvet* involving the Olympics.

+ *Casey's Shadow* (1978), about a boy who raises and trains a champion Quarter Horse.

+ *The Electric Horseman* (1979), about a rodeo cowboy who starred in Las Vegas.

+ *The Black Stallion* (1979), based on Walter Farley's book about a boy stranded on an island with a black horse.

+ *Wild Horse Hank* (1979), about a cowgirl attempting to save wild Mustangs from poachers.

+ *The Man from Snowy River* (1982), about an Australian and wild horses.

+ *Phar Lap* (1983), about the famous Australian racehorse.

+ *The Black Stallion Returns* (1983), a sequel to *The Black Stallion*, about a stolen stallion in the Middle East.

+ *Champions* (1984), about a cancer-stricken jockey who wanted to win the Grand National.

+ *Sylvester* (1985), about a girl training a bronco for jumping.

+ *Lady Hawke* (1985), a movie with a Friesian in the key role.

+ *Let It Ride* (1989), about betting on horse races.

+ *Wild Hearts Cannot Be Broken* (1991), a must-see film about an orphan girl and diving horses during the Depression.

+ *The Silver Stallion: King of the Wild Brumbies* (1993), about an Australian wild horse.

+ *Pursuit of Honor* (1995), about horse slaughter in the early 1900s.

+ *Something to Talk About* (1995), a film starring Julia Roberts as a breeder of show horses.

+ *Two Bits and Pepper* (1995), a comedy about talking horses that rescue kidnapped girls.

+ *Breaking Free* (1995), about a blind jumping horse.

+ *The Horse Whisperer* (1998), about a talented horseman who takes on a troubled family and their horse.

+ *Shergar* (1999), about an Irish Thoroughbred kidnapped by the Irish Republican Army.

+ *All the Pretty Horses* (2000), about a young Texas rancher heading for Mexico.

+ *Spirit: Stallion of the Cimarron* (2002), an animated film about a roaming stallion.

+ *Virginia's Run* (2002), about a teen raising a foal from the mare owned by her deceased mother.

+ *Seabiscuit* (2003), about the famous Thoroughbred racehorse.

+ *Hildago* (2004), the story of a Pony Express courier who travels to Arabia to race.

+ *Into the West* (2005), about Irish boys on an adventure on a mysterious horse.

+ *Dreamer* (2005), about the rescue and rehabilitation of a racehorse with a broken leg.

+ *The Colt* (2005), a civil war drama about a colt born in a cavalry unit.

+ *Flicka* (2006), about a girl and a wild horse.

Index

Credits

Key: *a* above; *b* below; *l* left; *r* right; *c* center

Breyer Model Horses (www.breyerhorses.com): 50ar

Corbis: 15; Federico Gambarini/epa 40a; Bettmann 54b, 132; Rolf Vennebernd/epa 77; Tom Nebbia 94; Arctic-Images 146b; Paul Almasy 174bl

Getty Images: Jamie Squire 176a

istockphoto: Ken Babione 18b; Roberto A. Sanchez 62bl; Nora Litzelman 62br; PhotoGen-X/LifeJourneys 63br; Baldur Tryggvason 75b, 78; ggodby 91b; ray roper 147cr; Tony Campbell 178al; Frank Zierlein 179b; Carmen Martinez Banús 183cr

Pam Kaster & Molly the Pony (www.bayouponytales.com & www.mollythepony.com): 157

Shannon Lawlor (www.shannonlawlor.com): 167

Miscellaneous: Jean Kraus 25al, *ac & ar*; Vassil 32ar; Luis H. Saldana 66br; Rafael Moreira 170br

Rex Features: SNAP 55b; Action Press 107a; Everett Collection 184b

Wes & Ronda Shafer of Smokin Acres, breeders of the grulla filly Smokin Cocoa Sandoll and other Foundation Quarter Horses (www.smokinacres.com): 53br

Shutterstock: Wendy Kaveney Photography 1, 127ar; Eline Spek 2, 19a, 133al; Alexander A. Khromstov 3, 10br; Eric Isselée 9, 29al, 52b, 61, 119 (horse), 162b; Jody Dingle 10al; Tomislav Forgo 10ar; Miguel Angel Salinas Salinas 10bl; Christos Georghiou 11a, 124; Joseph Gareri 11b; Lagui 12c; Kirsty Pargeter 12bl, 109b, 110cr, 183cl; szarzynski 13al; ariadna de raadt 13cr; Oshchepkov Dmitry 13bl; James Steidl 14al; NatUlrich 14 & 51 (music); Paul Laragy 16a; Denise Kappa 16b, 22 & 142 (fabric); MAT 17a, 32cl, 46, 73cr; Accent 17b; Vitezslav Halamka 19b; Melissa Dockstader 20a; tadija 20b; tbradford 21; David Franklin 22 (clipboard); Ovidiu Iordachi 23a; Stacey Bates 23c, 125al; Chen Ping Hung 24 (map); Yuen 24 (horses on map); Marlena Zagajewska 24b; Timur Kulgarin 25b; Marie Cloke 26a; Zuzule 26b, 44a; David S. Baker 27al; Mark R. 27c; Alan Egginton 28a; Hermann Danzmayr 28b; Thomas Barrat 29ar; Sharon Morris 29c, 36 (main), 129a, 158a; Abramova Kseniya 29bl, 92c (horse), 106, 128; George Bailey 30a; Beata Becla 30bl; Ramona Heim 30br, 69al; marilyn barbone 31; Dale A. Stork 32br, 68a, 155a; Joy Brown 33ar, 39br, 69 (main), 90r (horses); Christopher Meder 33cl; Rainbow 33bl; Petr Maček 34al; Clara Natoli 34cr; Andrei Nekrassov 35cr; ivanastar 35br; Alexander Drogaytsev 36bl; Stephanie Coffman 37bl, 53bc, 87al (horse), 118a;

Jeff Banke 39cl, 176b; markrhiggins 40br, 126; T.W. 41; Taolmor 42a, 57ar, 129b; Karen Givens 42b, 67ar, 139, 154a; Iakov Kalini 43al & 73ar (apples); Blaz Kure 43bl; verityjohnson 44br, 130b; Maria Bell 45a; Margo Harrison 45b, 60a, 86a; emmanuelle bonzami 48; catnap 49ar; 8045159901 49b; BVA 50al, 57b; Matthias Meckel 50b; Lorraine Swanson 51 (horse); Nikita Rogul 53ar, 163a; Carlos E. Santa Maria 54a; Victorian Traditions 57al; Laila Kazakevica 58a, 143b; Sandy Maya Matzen 58b; Ivonne Wierink 59b; Jonathan Heger 63bl; Lee O'Dell 64a; B. Speckart 64b, 85a; charles taylor 65a; Gilmanshin 65b; chen 66a & 89b (ballerinas); Pete Klinger 67bl; John Black 67bc; Sergey Chushkin 68c; marekuliasz 68b; Danilo Ascione 70b; Hector Joseph Luman 71al; iofoto 71bl; David Burrows 71br; tony spuria 72a; Alex Kotlov 74b; Linda Bucklin 75a, 93bl, 149a; Alexey Antipov 76al; svetlin rusev 76ar; Michelle Marsan 76bl; Uncle Gene 80al; JeremyRichards 80bl; volk65 82a; Gines Valera Marin 82br; Jean Frooms 83b; vitor costa 84cl; Colour 84cr; risteski goce 85b; Poprugin Aleksey 87al (frame); Izaokas Sapiro 87ar; Trutta55 87br; Eleanor 88bl; Marlies Krummen 89a; Peter Asprey 91a; B.G Smith 92l (pepper); Marcel Jancovic 93al; Terrence Meehan 95a; Paul Maguire 96al, 161al; Galushko Sergey 96ac; Kalmatsuy Tatyana 96ar; Alexia Khruscheva 96b, 154b; Terry Alexander 98a; Perry Correll 99a; Chris Hellyar 99b; Kamil Sobócki 100a; Gravicapa 100b; Rui Manuel Teles Gomes 101al; Ekaterina Pokrovskaya 101ar; Joe Gough 101b; Antonio V. Oquias 102al; Fedorov Oleksiy 102ar; Artsem Martysiuk 102bl; Feng Yu 102br, 142 (clipboard); Chepko Danil Vitalevich 103; Condor 36 104a; Robert Inglis 104b; David Kelly 105ar; Vinicius Tupinamba 105 (mosquitoes); vilena makarica 108a; StillFX 109al; Jenna Layne Voigt 109ar; robert paul van beets 110al; Kucherenko Olena 110cl, 119 (feathers); Ostanina Ekaterina Vadimovna 110bl Domenico Gelermo 110br; 7382489561 111 (main); Cora Reed 113a; Robynrg 113b; Döri O'Connell 114a; Thierry Dagnelie 114b; Johann Piber 115a; Kondrashov MIkhail Evgenevich 116al; Ron Hilton 116br; Heath Doman 117al; Timothy Large 117bl; Tatiana Morozova 118b; Claudia Steininger 120a; juliengrondin 120bl; Byron W. Moore 120br, 156b; Lena Lir 121a; Nancy Kennedy 121b; Tund 122b; Penelope Berger 123a, 174al; Morgan Lane Photography 125bl, 168; jocicalek 127cl; Adrian Lucki 127cr; Shpak Anton 127b; Dana Bartekoske 131al; Caroline Devulder 131 (ticks), 131bc; Oculo 131br; Cathleen Clapper 134; JustASC 136b; Johann Helgason 137, 159al; Mikhail Pogosov 138b; Dennis Cox 140b; acoi 141a; Winthrop Brookhouse 141b; ilker canikligil 143a; Nassyrov Ruslan 144bl; absolut 145a; Stephen Kiers 145b; Elena Kalistratova 146al; pixelman 146ar; Joy Miller 147al; Erik Lam 148br; Paul Paladin 148al; 1125089601 148bl; Lincoln Rogers 150ar, 165b; studio_chki 150bc; P. Uzunova 152a; Jovan Nikolic 152bl; Micha? Karbowiak 152br; Galyna Andrushko 153b; Holly Kuchera 156a; Michael Stokes 158b; Olemac 159br; nhtg 160al; J. Hindman 160br; Bruno Passigatti 161ar (mirror); Carolyne Pehora 161b; Nancy Tripp 162al; ikopylov 164al; Ross Wallace 164ar; Ismael Montero Verdu 164bl; Karen Hadley 170bl; Patrick Power 171l; Nigel Paul Monckton 172as; Sergey I 173av; nagib 173b; hadisagin 175a; Glenn Jenkinson 177a; Cheryl Kunde 177b; Tjerrie Smit 178br; Renee Keeton/Simply Focused Studios 179al; Geoffrey Kuchera 180r; Vincent Giordano 182al; David Hamman 182 (main); Kurilin Gennadiy Nikolaevich 183bl; OlgaLis 184a; thecarlinco 185b. Various background papers: emily2k; Perov Stanislav; Robyn Mackenzie; Lars Lindblad; javarman

TopFoto: ullsteinbild 169; Michael Geissinger/The Image Works 181

All other photographs and illustrations are the copyright of Quarto Publishing plc. While every effort has been made to credit contributors, Quarto would like to apologize should there have been any omissions or errors—and would be pleased to make the appropriate correction for future editions of the book.

AUTHOR'S ACKNOWLEDGMENTS

This book was written with the encouragement of my family, through whom I am most blessed: Susie, Genni, Carly, Lindsay, Jordan, Katie, Ryeanne, Cammie, and Brandie. I want to personally dedicate this book to them, their spouses, and my grandchildren. Special thanks and appreciation are due to my editor, Michelle Pickering, who was so efficient, creative, and professional in the book's production.